MASTERING
YOUR
EMOTIONS

WITH YOUR SPOUSE
AND OTHERS

D1565463

Seven Steps for Transforming
Emotional Reactivity

MASTERING YOUR EMOTIONS

WITH YOUR SPOUSE AND OTHERS

JIM PIEKARSKI
Marriage and Family Therapist

MASTERING YOUR EMOTIONS WITH YOUR SPOUSE AND OTHERS: *Seven Steps for Transforming Emotional Reactivity.*

Copyright 2012 by Jim Piekarski.

Contact the author at jim.piekarski@aol.com.

ISBN 978-0-615-69068-1

ACKNOWLEDGEMENTS

It takes many people to write a book. I would like to thank Cynthia TenEyck, Kay Lee, and Alicia Mitchell for their detailed editing of the manuscript. Alan Bleiman, Marcia Wall, Sarah Avery, Alicia Mitchell and Cecilia Kolonie are all therapists to whom I am grateful for reading the manuscript and giving me excellent feedback about its psychological content. I would also like to thank my significant other, Dr. Karen Hylen, and Tim Butler, MFT for their own long-time enthusiasm for these ideas and for our discussions over the years about emotional reactivity.

TABLE OF CONTENTS

INTRODUCTION

This book is the result of years of providing therapy to couples, families, and individuals in trouble with their relationships. When I began my practice, I noticed that people who displayed good communication skills in normal interactions with others could change drastically when they interacted with family members or their spouses. There was a distinct difference between how people acted when calm and how they acted when upset. People who become emotionally reactive, can't access communication skills. Emotional reactivity (ER) short-circuits a person's capacity to think clearly and act rationally. This is particularly true when a person is interacting with a loved one and has a history of emotional reactivity with that person. The main requirement in mastering one's emotions is to overcome emotional reactivity.

A couple that I worked with was a prime example of this. When calm, both the husband and wife communicated clearly and supported each other. It was obvious to me that both of them cared for each other and were highly committed to the relationship. This changed rapidly as soon as they brought up a topic with "history" around it. Their mood would change and within minutes they would be swearing at each other, and only with the greatest difficulty could I stop them from verbally abusing each other in my office. This couple exemplified the paradox that I was experiencing. How could I help people who could express themselves well when calm but then lose possession of themselves so thoroughly when upset? What made people be cruel to their loved ones despite their best intentions? Many of the people I treated tried to be more loving, but they were unable to respond differently even after learning state-of-the-art communication skills. Attempts to communicate about difficult issues would trigger strong emotions, the person would regress, and the communication skills that they knew would fly out the window.

This wasn't only a problem with my clients. I knew what it was like to try to communicate to a loved one and be surprised to find the communication burst into flames. My intention to discuss a problem would transform itself, and suddenly I would be defensive and angry. The love and compassion that I intended would evaporate in a storm of bad feeling—the whirlpool of emotional reactivity pulling me in, along with my spouse, or family member. I found it very frustrating. At first, I blamed the other person. "If only she weren't so irrational." "If he would just listen to what I had to say." It took me a while to realize it wasn't just the other person who was to blame, because I was participating in this insanity, too. When I became a therapist and saw this happening in my clients, it was familiar. I attempted to change this in myself by trying to use good communication skills and to look at past old wounds and understand how these were affecting my relationships. These skills worked great when my spouse and I were calm, but when we were upset these techniques helped only a little, if at all, because they did not deal with the basic problem. The problem was emotional—and not a set of emotions that were easily handled. It was an emotional reaction that was deep and primitive.

Emotions can be nebulous and hard to understand; their form being less distinct than the other two major areas of experience, thoughts and sensations. Until recently, psychotherapy focused on changing behavior or changing how we think about things. Although these therapy techniques help a person in a rational state of mind, it is rare for a person to successfully use them when emotionally reactive. I couldn't do it myself, and I didn't think my problem with emotional reactivity was any greater than that of my friends or clients.

I became interested in understanding emotional reactivity hoping to find a way to help myself and others prevent it from harming our relationships. I learned about the fight or flight response that occurs in a part of the brain that is responsible for instinctive self-protection which is different from the part of the brain that learns skills. Common rational solutions were not sufficient; a different focus was necessary to deal with this problem. At the time I was practicing mindfulness and meditation which I found to be of great benefit, because within a few minutes of mindfulness practice I experienced a sense of calm and centeredness. After practicing mindfulness it became harder for me to be emotionally reactive, and I wanted to share this with my clients. I began introducing mindfulness into therapy and I was gratified to see that it was immediately helpful to clients who were motivated to practice it.

Although the practice of mindfulness was generally helpful, I wanted to develop a way to apply it specifically to interpersonal reactivity. To make it easy for my clients to manage their emotions, I created a simple step-by-step process that focused mindfulness and other techniques directly on emotional reactivity. This would help clients to understand their emotional reactivity, gain control of it, and once again restore love and compassion to their relationships. This combination of focusing directly on the problem of emotional reactivity and the practice of mindfulness had improved my ability to contain my emotional reactivity. Every relationship in my life improved.

I was very pleased with the results in my practice. Once clients understood the trap they were caught in and given a step-by-step understanding of how to get out of it, they made surprising progress. It is amazing what people can do when they truly understand a problem and have a clear plan to overcome it. I found that couples, families, and individuals all benefited from the approach.

In the last fifteen years therapists have been using mindfulness as a primary psychological tool and are getting results. However, most psychological techniques and programs designed to help people handle their emotions are for those with serious psychological diagnoses, such as borderline personality disorder. But everybody becomes emotionally reactive at times, not just people with severe problems. Presented here is a clear and simple approach for normal people to manage the emotions that come up in interpersonal situations.

Emotional reactivity must be understood clearly in order to deal with it effectively. It tends to disguise itself as other issues. When people do not recognize it, they often blame their interpersonal problems on other people. There are two levels of communication: the logical, language-based level and the emotional level. People communicate emotionally all the time, however, most people are not fully aware of it. Their attention remains on the level of words and they do not realize that the emotional level of communication is stronger and can take over the direction of communication entirely. Inattention to the emotional level of communication is an important reason that people have conflict in relationship.

Folklore says that discovering a devil's name gives you power over it. One illustration of this is the folktale, *Rumpelstiltskin*. When the queen speaks the name Rumpelstiltskin, his evil power disappears and the queen's child is returned to her. Likewise, once we gain an understanding of emotional reactivity, and can identify it in ourselves, then we can take steps towards change.

It was in marital counseling that I first began to see the need for couples to transform their emotional reactivity. As an inexperienced therapist, I encouraged couples to use the common techniques for improving communication, problem-solving, and changing behaviors. However, a couple's emotional reactivity could easily interrupt their attempts to apply these new skills. I was trying to treat the emotional level of communication with techniques designed to work with the rational level. Emotional reactivity is regressive; it takes people back to a more primitive level of functioning, creating more problems and inhibiting positive change.

With couples, a strategy and a set of methods to help them deal with emotional reactivity are crucial to resolving marital problems.

The methods presented here are not new and are taken from many schools of psychotherapy. The concept that is new is the focus on emotional reactivity and on what tools are needed to tame this central problem in relationships. This focus helps people identify what the problems really are and to then take responsibility for them. Once a person realizes that ER inhibits their capacity to experience long-term love in their lives, he or she becomes very motivated to change. Although the skills for overcoming emotional reactivity are highly effective for couples, they benefit individuals and families as well.

To be able to change our emotional reactivity, we need to understand it and then be very attentive to how it manifests in our lives. It is important to make our own discoveries, because to accept the information without seeing how it operates in our lives will be insufficient. Habits of mind and emotion are very difficult to break, because these habits are built up and practiced over many years. The good news is that fixing these bad habits doesn't have to take as long as their development. We can change emotional reactivity in a relatively short time, if we are determined and follow the steps outlined in this book.

This book outlines an approach designed for the average person who has trouble with emotional reactivity—the person who occasionally gets their buttons pushed by others or the person who has one or two relationships that trigger difficult emotions. Here is a step-by-step method of transforming emotional reactivity into responses that are more fruitful and caring. It provides a path to end the dysfunctional triggering of the fight-or-flight reaction and is a step on the path of mastering your emotions. I hope that you can benefit from these techniques as I and many others have done.

Steps to Overcoming Emotional Reactivity

This book is designed to take you through the steps that will help you master emotional reactivity. The first section of the book (Chapters 2-7) explores the techniques that are effective in reducing ER and getting relationships back in good working order. Chapter One defines and describes emotional reactivity and how it occurs in various relationships and guides you in distinguishing emotional reactivity from healthy emotions.

Chapter Two describes methods to stop externalizing problems and for setting good boundaries. Because emotionally reactive people project blame onto others and the environment, they miss the opportunity to make changes in themselves. Chapter Three demonstrates how to develop the level of commitment necessary to be successful in overcoming this difficult problem. Building motivation is an essential step before beginning this important endeavor. Chapter Four focuses on behaviors that are triggered by emotional reactivity and how these must be stopped so more functional behaviors can be adopted. The central theme is improving communication, since the most common emotionally reactive behavior is hurtful communication.

Chapter Five describes how to handle the high emotional arousal that often accompanies emotional reactivity. These techniques, based on the Buddhist concept of mindfulness, are critical in dealing with strong emotions and enable us to remain centered enough to handle situations appropriately. Chapter Six discusses how distortions in thinking contribute to emotional reactivity, and how to change the distortions so that one is thinking more clearly. Chapter Seven demonstrates how these basic exercises can be integrated into a set of coping skills through practice. Chapter Eight presents methods to reduce emotional reactivity and respond more compassionately with loved ones.

The second part of the book investigates aspects of emotions that are helpful to understand in applying the steps in the first part of the book. Chapters Nine, Ten and Eleven provide a deeper understanding of emotions. Chapter Nine breaks down emotions into five basic components, an approach that eliminates much of the confusion commonly experienced when trying to understand the realm of emotions. The steps for transforming emotional reactivity described in the first half of this book are based on this five-component model of emotion. Some of the specific causes of emotional reactivity are described in Chapter Ten, imparting a greater knowledge of how your own emotional reactivity may have developed. Chapter Eleven explores how the fear of uncomfortable feelings is not only a cause of emotional reactivity but may be the root of other psychological problems. Chapter Twelve, the final chapter, explores emotional reactivity and its relevance to therapy and healing in general. Transforming emotional reactivity has great therapeutic value beyond helping to negotiate relationships.

CHAPTER 1

What is Emotional Reactivity

"A life of reaction is a life of slavery, intellectually and spiritually. One must fight for a life of action, not reaction."

RITA MAE BROWN

Emotional reactivity is one of the most serious and destructive problems that occur in relationships, and it short-circuits our ability to compassionately respond to our loved ones. In a marriage, it leads to unhappiness and divorce. When it occurs in a family, it creates conflict and leaves our children a legacy of emotional problems. When we are emotionally reactive, communication is disrupted and feelings of intimacy evaporate. Emotional reactivity (ER) arises in all kinds of relationships: between parents and children, among family members and friends, romantic relationships, and even in business relationships. Unfortunately, it tends to be most potent with our closest and most cherished relationships transforming a relationship that was once loving

1

and respectful into one full of anger and frustration. Ultimately, it can lead to alienation and separation.

Murray Bowen, considered to be one of the "fathers" of family therapy, originally coined the term "emotional reactivity." He saw that there was strong reactivity between members of troubled families, and he felt that a person's ability to handle reactivity was a prime indicator of how healthy one could be in a relationship. He observed that people's anxiety levels increased dramatically when they were emotionally reactive and understood that our ability to think things through rationally and to problem-solve is severely compromised when in this state.

We experience emotional reactivity when somebody "pushes our buttons" and we emotionally overreact to another person, event, or situation. Emotional reactivity is the inability to handle our emotions well. When we are emotionally reactive we act against our best interests—saying and doing things that we regret. ER is in no way helpful to us. It doesn't aid us in resolving real problems because it is based on a distorted view of events. Although it can look similar, it differs from the expression of healthy emotions. When not dealt with, it can invade our relationships and replace loving feelings with those of anger, resentment, fear, and hurt.

Two pathways exist for communication between people—through reason and through emotion. The rational pathway uses language and logic. We put ideas into words and try to communicate them to others. This pathway works well when we are calm and not too emotional. When we get emotional the rational pathway gets short-circuited.

We then no longer respond to the words that are being said; we react to the emotion that is being expressed. Strong emotion triggers our fight-or-flight reaction. This is governed by a very primitive part of the brain that signals danger to us. At this point we no longer pay attention to words and logic. We pay attention to the emotions being expressed and we automatically react to these emotions.

Most people are not aware of the distinctness of these two separate communication pathways. This puts them at a great disadvantage when dealing with emotional reactivity. The skills necessary to master the emotional level of communication are not well known and are very different from those we usually use in our interactions with others. Trying to apply "reasonable" methods to the emotionally reactive state does not work. Logic does not remedy the disruptions in the emotional level of communication. The focus of this book is to help readers master the techniques that can be directly used to repair this second, hidden level of communication—the emotional level.

Here is an example of how emotional reactivity may become so severe that the family was compelled to seek therapy. David notices that his daughter, Megan, did not arrive home directly from school as she promised she would. This issue has come up before. David asks her where she has been and why she was not home on time. His angry tone of voice indicates that his emotional reactivity is already triggered, and this is immediately communicated to Megan. Instead of listening to her Dad and his complaint, Megan becomes defensive and offers arguments and excuses for not coming home on time. Sue, Megan's mother, hears the conflict in the living room and finds it very disturbing. She comes to Megan's rescue. It upsets her to hear David talking to the children in such an angry manner. Even though she agrees with David's point about coming home late, David's anger alarms her and she becomes protective of Megan. When Sue starts defending Megan, David's anger rises, and he starts feeling hopeless. He feels that Sue never supports him in setting limits for the children. Justin, Megan's older brother, hears all this from his bedroom. He planned to go out in an hour to visit with friends, but he flees the house early to avoid experiencing these unpleasant emotions. All four members of this family are mired in a bog of unconscious emotional reactions, and this triggers everybody to behave in a way contrary to family love and cooperation. The contagious character of emotional reactivity is destructive to David and Sue's marriage, their relationship with their children, and to the children's development.

David and Sue are trying their best. They are focused on doing what they think is right yet are unable to see that their emotional reactivity is the source of their problems. David is determined to focus on setting limits for the children; Sue is concerned about protecting the children from David's anger; Megan feels assaulted and is trying to defend herself; and Justin wants to protect his peace of mind by escaping from the situation. Each person tries to take action in a way that they believe will relieve their pain, but they are caught in a web of unconscious reactions that none of them understands. These reactions disrupt the family bonds and undermine the natural love and compassion this family normally feels. Because of emotional reactivity, the parents are unable to deal successfully with Megan's tardiness, only creating more pain for each other.

Nobody in the family understands that their problem lies on the emotional pathway of communication rather than the rational one. David is reacting to a history of power struggles with Megan. Otherwise, the current incident would not have made him so angry. Megan reacts to David's anger rather than his request to come home on time. She feels compelled to "stand up for herself" and not let David "lord it over her". She creates a wall of stubbornness and refuses to follow the rules. Susan's fear for her daughter gets triggered and she argues with David even though she is in agreement with him logically about the importance of setting limits. Justin's logic tells him there is no point in leaving early to go to his friend's house, but the anxiety triggered by the family fight is so painful he removes himself to feel better.

Each person in the family seeks a rational explanation for what is going on in the family and for their own behavior. They miss what is actually driving these events—the emotional exchange between each person. Because they define the problem in the wrong way, none of them are able to find a solution to the conflict.

Couples and families that have problems also have high levels of emotional reactivity. Serious problems in relationships and high levels of emotional reactivity occur together. If there is an ongoing issue in a relationship that remains unresolved for a period of time, sooner or later the frustration may trigger emotional reactivity leading to additional problems. If emotional reactivity is present, it needs to be dealt with first. It causes too much confusion and upset between people. ER disrupts clear thinking and triggers poor communication and behavior. The cooperative spirit necessary for resolving other problems is lost.

Because ER is so disruptive to communication and happiness, it is mandatory that people deal with their emotional reactivity as one of the primary steps in their efforts to resolve their problems. Once the individuals gain a foothold in dealing with their ER, then progress in other areas can be made much more easily. Often, when a couple or family reduces their emotional reactivity, their harmony and loving feelings automatically return and little else needs to be done. Those who were emotionally reactive had the verbal skills; they just couldn't use them when they were so upset.

Emotional reactivity has many things in common with the concept of flooding, which was measured in couples by Dr John Gottman in his studies on marriage. Gottman found that people who become flooded with emotion get angry, or shut down, because their intense confusion and overwhelming distress trigger emotional reactivity. When swept away by this flood of emotion, it is natural to want to shut down to avoid these painful feelings. Either the flooding reaction itself or the attempts to avoid it create distance in our relationships.

Having the ability to handle emotional reactivity is one of the components of what Daniel Goleman describes as "emotional intelligence" in his book by that name. Goleman writes that the skill most necessary for success – even more necessary than a high I.Q.–is the ability to handle emotions well. Murray Bowen saw the level of ER as inversely related to the health of a family or couple. The higher the emotional reactivity the more disturbed the family or couple, and the more difficult it was for them to resolve their problems. Families and couples with low levels of emotional reactivity are healthier, and they demonstrate more capacity to resolve differences that naturally occur in relationships. Bowen was also observant in understanding that emotional reactivity is not just getting angry. It also includes many other emotions as well as avoidant behaviors.

By identifying and understanding the concept of emotional reactivity, we may learn what goes wrong in our relationships with others and how to bridge the gap between the world of emotion and the world of interpersonal relationships. We may then be able to understand many things about our relationships that were hidden from us before and gain insight into developing ways of coping with ER when it occurs.

The Physiological Basis of Emotional Reactivity

The sympathetic nervous system is the basis of emotional reactivity. It is the part of our autonomic nervous system that is responsible for our fight-or-flight reactions that often occur when situations are viewed as threatening. In relationships these reactions may manifest themselves as arguments or conflict on one hand, or as avoidance and shutting down on the other. Emotionally, the fight reaction corresponds to feelings of anger, hatred and annoyance. Underlying the flight reactions are feelings of fear, dread and anxiety.

The fight-or-flight reaction's innate purpose is to act as a defense mechanism and protect us from danger. There is nothing wrong with this reaction in its pure form. When we need to physically protect ourselves or run away from danger, our emotions shoot adrenaline into our system so that we may respond quickly, decisively and with strength. This purely physiological defense is a necessity and not the problem. Problems arise when other parts of our brain are stimulated by the fight-or-flight reaction. When this happens, distorted thoughts come into our minds, and habitual behaviors that are not practical for the situation express themselves. Our dysfunctional learning from poor upbringing or past traumatic events gets activated.

In animals, a fight-or-flight response of the sympathetic nervous system is obvious from the animal's behavior–an animal either fights or runs away. These behaviors in animals are simpler than in humans. Because of our capacity for thinking and social conditioning, the behaviors associated with the fight-or-flight reaction are more complicated. After all, we react to family members or others that are important to us in some way and with whom we are emotionally involved. This causes us to want to mask our emotions from others to protect the relationship or sometimes to even hide these emotions from ourselves. Emotionally reactive behaviors may become quite complex and easily overlooked when they occur in relationships with those we want to love and protect. Although there are many ways for people to express their emotional reactivity, there are three common patterns: through conflict, avoidance, or caretaking.

The "Fight" Reaction

The conflict side of the fight-or-flight syndrome is usually the easiest to distinguish and the most obvious to outsiders. Adrenaline and other hormones are triggered in our bodies. We raise our voices, get agitated, and strike out at the other person, usually verbally.

Aaron is with his girlfriend Rebecca at a friend's party. Rebecca is getting attention from other men at the party. Aaron tries to ignore this. However, when the couple leave the party and are alone in the car, Aaron explodes and accuses Rebecca of encouraging other men to flirt with her. Rebecca feels this is unfair because she tried her best to put these admirers off politely and quickly. Aaron persists in his recriminations toward Rebecca. She finally blows up saying to Aaron derogatory things about his manhood and lack of confidence. Both Aaron and Rebecca have given in to their emotional reactivity by getting angry. Aaron holds his feelings back until he gets into the car. Rebecca tries to avoid getting emotionally reactive, but Aaron's accusations finally get to her until she blows up also. They end up feeling distressed and distant from each other. This is a common example of how one person may work himself into an emotionally reactive state until someone close to him is enticed to join in. Aaron persisted with his emotional reactivity long enough to trigger Rebecca.

In another example, Sarah has been vying with a fellow employee, Karen, for a position that is opening up in their company. When Karen gets the position, Sarah starts badmouthing Karen to nearly everybody she talks to. Although Sarah knows she is being unfair and is making herself seem petty, she somehow feels compelled to continue her negative comments. Sarah is possessed by her emotional reactivity. She does not directly confront Karen, but her anger is used in an indirect manner to try to damage Karen's reputation. She appears calm when criticizing Karen because she wants to appear more objective, but her anger and disappointment in the job loss comes out obliquely in her efforts to cast stones at Karen.

Avoidance or Flight Response

Most people express their emotional reactivity through either direct or indirect conflict. Direct conflict is expressed by lashing out at someone in an inappropriate and angry manner, causing damage in a relationship. A great many people, however, express their emotional reactivity through avoidant behaviors. Bowen was observant in understanding that emotional reactivity also includes avoidant behaviors and efforts to shut down and remain calm at all costs. The avoidant person has learned that direct conflict is painful, they feel uncomfortable with anger, or they fear the damage that might occur to their relationships. They avoid open conflict and do not resort to it unless they feel like they have no choice, and they shy away from other unwanted emotions such as guilt, humiliation, sadness, shame or fear. These behaviors are difficult to identify in ourselves and in others because they are more subtle than open conflict.

Avoidant behaviors are anticipatory. We may know certain events to be troublesome or painful emotionally, so we find ways to avoid them before they occur. There are three basic ways that we avoid issues. The first is something that was recorded by John Gottman in his work with couples, called "stonewalling," which he found to be more common in men. When confronted by their wives in certain situations, husbands would experience strong sympathetic reactions, sometimes having their heart rates increase by over 30 beats per minute. They would shut themselves down by dissociating from the situation to protect themselves from over-stimulation. This emotional withdrawal from the relationship was shown to be damaging to marriages and was what Gottman described as one of four destructive communication sequences in a marriage.

The second common mode of avoidance is through anticipation. We anticipate that conflict will occur in a situation and avoid it before it happens. Sometimes, we already have begun to feel the uncomfortable emotion and we try to run away from or distract ourselves from this discomfort. The ways in which this can be done are numerous. One common way is to avoid certain topics of conversation. Through consistent interaction with another person we become aware of those "hot" topics that lead to conflict and bad feelings. We avoid discussing the difficult areas in our relationships. An example of this on a social level is the injunction to not bring up topics of religion and politics in polite society. We know that for many people these topics may trigger emotional reactivity.

What are avoiders avoiding? There are two basic things. One is the possible injury to a relationship that emotional reactivity can cause, such as when people do not speak to each other for years due to an

11

angry incident or outburst. Some relationships are very difficult to repair after an angry confrontation when nasty things are said. The second basic thing that avoiders fear is the feeling of being flooded with negative emotions that cause a high level of distress. These people automatically avoid this sense of discomfort even when it may be in their best interest to face the emotion. Avoiders fear the breakdown in their relationships and they hate to feel vulnerable or out of control emotionally.

John is a newly recovered alcoholic. After being sober for two months, he decided to go out to his first recovery dance. Everybody there is sober and appears to be having fun. John asks a woman to dance and she refuses. He asks another and she refuses also. Even though they both refuse nicely, an intense feeling of humiliation begins to sweep over John, because he takes the rejection very personally. He concludes that he is different than everybody else and does not belong. He imagines that everybody at the dance is aware of his humiliation, so he leaves the dance and drives straight to his old bar and orders a drink, knowing that alcohol will numb his feeling of humiliation. John has become emotionally reactive in this situation and this becomes his trigger for relapse.

John demonstrates avoidance of a strong emotional state that he experiences as unpleasant. He has an emotionally reactive response because he does not deal with his emotions in a healthy manner. John triggers his emotional reactivity on his own. No angry persona is necessary to trigger him. His own distorted thoughts trigger his fight-or-flight. Usually, we need to be interacting with another person who is emotionally reactive to get such a strong avoidant response. Unfortunately, John's efforts to avoid a situation he sees as humiliating lead to his return to drinking.

Carol is making dinner while Ted is sitting on the couch watching sports. She is upset that Ted I does not ask if she needs help with dinner. Because she has brought this issue up in the past, and it has always led to unpleasant feelings of anger, she avoids saying anything for fear of causing another argument. The resentment is buried, but it does not go away, adding to a feeling of distance from Ted. Based on past experiences of anger and frustration with Ted, Carol avoids the situation and tries to stuff her feelings.

Fear of dealing with our feelings is a much more common problem than is usually understood. Fear plays a significant part in many mental health problems and a major role in emotional reactivity.

Caretaking

Similar to avoidance or flight reactions, the act of caretaking is the third type of emotionally reactive behavior. Here the person tries to deflect difficulties in relationships and avoid conflict by focusing positive attention on the other person before the other person has a chance to get upset. Whenever there is a sense of distance in the relationship, the caretaker immediately moves to soothe the other's feelings and goes to great lengths to make sure that nobody gets angry or upset. The caretaking person can also be unduly afraid that something bad will happen to their loved one. This fear can be so great that it overrides more rational assessments of the loved one's plight.

Caretaking is one of the behaviors that make up the phenomena labeled codependency. Codependency describes a set of behaviors exhibited by people who are close to those with addiction problems. Codependent behavior is destructive to caretakers as well as to those who suffer from addiction. Caretakers lose themselves in their efforts to influence their loved ones, yet enable their loved ones to continue their addictions.

You don't need an addict in your life to be a caretaker; caring for others can be a good and helpful service. But, there is a difference between "caring" for someone and "caretaking" that person. Caretaking is an extreme—leading people to behaviors that are compulsive and harmful to the individuals involved. Caring is based on love and concern for the other. Caretaking may soothe things in the short run, but it damages relationships in the long run. It is based on guilt, the fear of conflict or some other uncomfortable emotion, whereas the motivating force behind caring is love. Sometimes, the only way for us to tell the difference between caring and caretaking is to check our intentions. Are we really trying to benefit the other person or are we just trying to make bad feelings go away?

Sometimes caretakers lose themselves so completely in others that they no longer know what they feel, think, or want themselves. Their radar is so sensitive to the needs of others that they forget to pay attention to their own needs. They find ways to make themselves indispensable to others, thereby assuring themselves a place in the other person's life. Asserting themselves and making waves can be frightening for them so they forgo fulfilling their own needs to avoid conflict or abandonment.

Sally is very tuned in to the needs of others. She spends many hours per day doing kind deeds for her friends and family, and sometimes anticipates others' needs long before they do themselves. Her giving is not selfless, however. Because few people are willing to give back as much as she gives, Sally begins to feel resentment towards them. Her son, Alan, is sixteen, and she can't stand to see him upset. When she sees that he might be getting upset or uncomfortable, she immediately soothes him by giving him what he wants. Unfortunately, this has backfired; Alan has learned that if he becomes more and more demanding, he gets what he wants.

Because Sally protects Alan from dealing with internal feelings of frustration, Alan has no chance to develop much tolerance for frustration in his life. He wants what he wants when he wants it. He begins to use drugs and alcohol to soothe himself and to avoid any uncomfortable feelings. He is sure that his mother will continue to save him from the negative consequences of his choices, because she always comes to his rescue.

Sally is confused. She feels she has been a very loving and giving mother, and she finds it hard to understand why her son is having so much trouble. Sally does not realize that her desperate efforts to avoid conflict have hindered the expression of love toward her son and have stolen Alan's opportunity to learn to deal with his own feelings of discomfort.

Jamie worked in a drug and alcohol halfway house and was highly competent at her job. She was able to balance her compassion for clients with the ability to establish firm limits. Her fellow workers admired her dedication and skill in supporting others through their recovery. When her nineteen-year-old son, Adam, began using drugs, however, she was at a loss as to how to handle this. The skills that she exhibited in managing the recovering people in her job were not available to her with her son's problems. The fear that he might overdose or be arrested clouded her judgment. She found it very hard to set limits with him and this codependency enabled him to take advantage of her financially. Her guilt about breaking up with his father when he was younger also affected her. Jamie's fear and guilt dominated her, making it difficult for her to access the skills in the rational part of her mind. Luckily, Jamie had good friends in Alcoholics Anonymous who provided guidance on how to deal with her son. They reminded her of the skills she had and encouraged her to not surrender to her fears.

These general ways of expressing emotional reactivity are common to us all. We probably have done all of them at some point in our lives. However, we usually develop a personality style based upon the expression with which we are most comfortable. Some people are comfortable with the fight part of the fight/flight response. These people confront things directly. Anger, however, can easily interfere with their ability to handle situations successfully. When we get flooded with anger, we tend not to think clearly. It becomes more difficult to handle things appropriately. People who allow anger to overtake them also may trigger a strong fight-or-flight response in others. Some people even get addicted to this angry state of mind and feel compelled to draw others into the swirl of emotional reactivity with them.

Avoidance, or flight, can be adopted into a personality style, too. Because avoidant people have such a strong distaste for conflict or for being upset, their capacity for avoidance may become habitual and extreme. They may learn to avoid situations that might cause themselves discomfort, usually, by being adept at excuses. "I don't want to go to that party because I have nothing to wear." "There is no point in telling him the truth. He would just get angry and wouldn't listen to me anyway." The excuses become justifications for avoidance. Their lives can become very circumscribed, causing them to only participate in activities that are routine and to avoid taking risks in other areas.

Caretaking behaviors may become so ingrained that they become part of one's personality style. Caretakers develop relationships based on their ability to be needed. They often choose people who are disadvantaged so that they will be indispensable to them. Their whole lives may revolve around their roles as caretakers, instead of enjoying relationships in which they could get help or support for themselves.

The different ways of expressing emotional reactivity – whether by a fight or flight reaction, avoidance or caretaking–may become habitual over time. These traits are usually developed early in childhood in reaction to the emotional reactivity in the family.

A Dysfunctional Expression of Emotions

Emotional reactivity must be distinguished from the healthy expression of emotions. Emotions are necessary for us and have many positive functions in our lives. Anger helps us stand up for ourselves. Fear keeps us away from danger. Grief helps us recognize our love for others and helps us move on after a loss. We need to experience our emotions to remain healthy, psychologically and physically. (As we will see in Chapter Ten, awareness of emotions and their healthy expression are of primal importance to our functioning.) When our emotions are expressed in a direct and healthy manner, we are less emotionally reactive. Emotional reactivity is a type of emotional response—but a distorted, dysfunctional one that is very different than the healthy expression of emotions.

Emotional reactivity can be distinguished from healthy emotion in four basic ways. Both emotional reactivity and emotion can have strong feeling components. The difference is that emotional reactivity has negative behavior that accompanies it. This behavior is habitual and tends to be counterproductive. Because the behavior that occurs when we are emotionally reactive is habitual, rather than consciously chosen for the situation, it can get us into trouble and is not in our best interest.

Many people confuse emotional reactivity with being in touch with one's "true feelings." It is essential that we be able to tell the difference between the two. Sometimes, people caught in this misunderstanding defend their emotional reactivity by saying, "I have a right to express my emotions," or "It's important for me to get my feelings out." They haven't yet learned that emotional reactivity is a type of confusion that stops us from handling our emotions in a healthy manner. Alternately, people who are confused by the difference between healthy emotions and emotional reactivity may repress their true feelings. Because they have experienced emotional reactivity so often in their relationships, they fear that emotional expression leads to conflict and alienation. This person does not realize that there is a healthy way to express emotions that leads to better communication and greater intimacy. The intention of the information presented here is to help people reduce emotional reactivity and at the same time to preserve or improve the natural expression of healthy emotion.

Emotional reactivity reduces our capacity to be flexible in our behavior and to make good choices in how to express our emotions. For instance, grief over the loss of a loved one is a natural emotion whose expression is important for us. Its full expression helps us experience the loss and move on with our lives. An emotionally reactive expression of grief causes us to not only feel sad but to do something destructive as a result of our grief. An example is a person who loses a loved one and deals with it by using drugs. This goes beyond the normal expression of grief into the realm of destructive behavior. We can lose control of our behavior when we are emotionally reactive, and we act in a way that is destructive to ourselves, to others, or to the relationships we are a part of. The most typical negative behavior that people exhibit when they are emotionally reactive is hurtful communication. The triggering of negative behavior is the first way to distinguish emotional reactivity from healthy emotion.

The second way that emotional reactivity is different from a healthy response is the distortions that occur in our thinking when emotions take over. When ER is strong, we do not see things clearly.

Our mind jumps in and distorts what is really happening. Jill lost her boyfriend. She not only feels sadness with this loss, which is natural, but she also believes that she will never find anybody else in her life and will end up all alone. For her, this distorted belief changes her sadness into depression.

Another distinction between ER and healthy emotions is that ER is based on past habits and experiences projected onto present situations. When Bob's wife, Anne, complains to him, Bob reacts with strong defensiveness. His mother was critical of him when he was growing up. Anne's simple complaints trigger this pain from his childhood, causing him to become emotionally reactive. Unresolved hurts from the past may resurface when triggered by situations that look similar in the present.

Lastly, the reactions of ER are different from those of a healthy emotion because they are out of proportion to the stimulus that triggers the reaction. When Bob reacts to Anne in the above example, he reacts almost violently to a simple complaint. His reaction is much more intense than the stimulus demands. Healthy emotions have an expression that is much more in line with the intensity of the stimulus. Even very powerful emotions like intense anger are not necessarily emotionally reactive and can be appropriate for the stimulus. If someone attacks us physically, we may become very angry and even violent in our efforts to protect ourselves. This response is in line with the intensity of the stimulus and is not emotional reactivity.

Here is an example that distinguishes between emotional reactivity and the healthy expression of emotion. Gina wants to talk about something that is bothering her and she is very upset, but her husband, Al, wants to avoid talking about it. He is afraid that discussing this issue with Gina will make her become emotionally dependent upon him. This is what happened when he listened to his mother's problems. She would cry on his shoulder and expect him to comfort her. This was very burdensome for Al.

Al demonstrates all four of the characteristics of emotional reactivity in his reaction to Gina. His behavior is destructive to the relationship, his view of the situation is distorted, that view is based on difficulties from the past, and he reacts in a manner that is out of proportion to the immediate situation. If Al were not emotionally reactive in this situation, his natural emotions of love and nurturing would be able to express themselves. He could listen to Gina and be able to comfort her. He would be capable of a compassionate response.

Relationships and Emotional Reactivity

In troubled marriages and relationships, emotional reactivity most often is the central problem. It poisons relationships, keeping many couples from having constructive discussions or finding solutions to their difficulties. These couples demonstrate that ER is "catching" – when one person is triggered, the other reacts accordingly–and their capacity for dealing with other problems diminishes rapidly. They must first deal with their emotions before they can make any progress on other issues. As their emotional reactivity increases, the amount of time they feel distress increases, which may be fifty per cent or more of the time they spend together. These two people who love each other wonder where the peace and joy that they once had together has gone; they don't realize that emotional reactivity is the villain in their relationship.

One couple seen in therapy was emotionally reactive about religion; she is a devout Catholic and he is an agnostic. Whenever they raised this issue, tempers flared, and their respectful and loving behavior disappeared. This couple could become quite verbally abusive to each other. They had to take responsibility and commit to facing their own emotional reactivity. This was a difficult change in perspective for them because they were used to blaming each other. However, after being confronted with their own unhappiness and their limited success in getting each other to change, they began to see how emotional reactivity was the major obstacle to their happiness.

As they identified and took responsibility for their ER, this couple began to move very quickly in resolving their problems. At the same time that their relationship improved, it became apparent that they had changed and matured in ways that went far beyond resolving their relationship difficulties. They became more productive, responsive and less reactive in other areas of their lives by accepting and transforming their emotional reactivity. Making this commitment to change helped them access and resolve personal issues that had plagued them both since childhood.

Emotionally reactive people have a hard time recognizing what is causing their problems. As couples come to understand their emotional reactivity and its negative consequences, and are given clear steps for managing their emotions, they may improve their relationships. When both partners tackle their ER, they make surprisingly rapid progress. There is a magic that occurs when people grasp what the real problem is that is creating so much difficulty. This progress can be so profound that it leads to deep changes in both individuals involved in the relationship.

These methods are not only helpful for couples, but individuals may benefit from them, also. Many people in individual therapy want to discuss the difficulties they are having in their relationships. Combating emotional reactivity offers these individuals a means to improve themselves that directly benefits the happiness they experience with loved ones. Individuals frequently react to their relationships, and these reactions provide an excellent opportunity to do this work.

Parent-child Relationships

Another type of relationship in which emotional reactivity commonly occurs is one between a parent and child. Many parents and children, when discussing certain issues, immediately experience emotional reactivity. For example, Rich is a teenager who wants to get his tongue pierced. He keeps mentioning it to Vickie, his mother—badgering her about it. She can no longer stand talking about it, and he hopes to wear her down so she'll say "yes." After a while there is so much emotional reactivity between them that mother and son can no longer discuss the issue reasonably, and the atmosphere between them is poisoned emotionally.

This is very common within families. As the emotional reactivity is expressed over time, each person in the family learns how the others react when they are upset, thus leading to a strong reactivity in these emotionally-trying interactions. Communication shuts down because people become touchy about certain subjects. The message is "don't talk to me about this."

Some family members learn to manipulate others through emotional reactivity–they learn how to push guilt or fear "buttons" to get what they want. Knowing that their family member will give them what they want when they do this, they will do it more. If we learn to transform our emotional reactivity, these manipulations will fall on deaf ears. People will give up manipulating when they find that it no longer works.

"Catching" Emotional Reactivity

There is a concept in psychology called *sympathetic induction*, meaning that emotions are contagious. If we are around someone who is laughing and joking, usually we will partake in the humor, also. If a sad person is talking to us and crying, we feel sadness ourselves. When someone else's fight-or-flight reaction is triggered, it affects us physically. When we hear someone yelling in our vicinity, our bodies immediately go into alert mode and our own fight-flight response becomes triggered. We may respond to this physiological triggering with emotional reactivity.

No matter where ER occurs it is catching. A typical example of the communicability of ER is in relationships where one person becomes verbally abusive and the other person responds in turn. This may occur in many situations—from arguments in families to arguments across the aisle in the U.S. Senate because the other person's anger is perceived as a threat. Unless one has learned to handle one's own arousal effectively, one may "catch" the emotional reactivity of another person.

Although emotional reactivity is contagious, the actual emotions experienced and behaviors expressed may differ significantly in each person. Each person may have a different response to being upset. A husband may immediately start caretaking his wife when she gets angry. Another person, in response to anger, may immediately leave the scene or shut down. A wife may get very upset over her husband's avoidant responses. Everybody reacts a bit differently, but no matter how the emotional reactivity is communicated, a disruption in intimacy or communication occurs.

Generations of Emotional Reactivity

Although emotional reactivity is a very common experience in families, it is far from being a benign experience. Its presence damages the whole family and is painful to everyone involved. It is especially traumatic for children who may be inhibited from developing emotionally.

Bowen says that emotional reactivity is passed down from parents to children and the children end up with the same level of emotional reactivity as the parents. This conditioning takes place through numerous incidents while the children are growing up. The particular child may not express the ER in the same manner as the parents, but the level of emotional reactivity will be similar. If a boy has a father who expresses his ER in a very angry manner, the boy may learn to avoid such angry outbursts at all costs. He may become very avoidant of conflict. How the child expresses his emotional reactivity depends not only on what he sees in the parent but on the child's genetic predisposition and what works for him.

The expression of emotional reactivity is particularly noticeable when children become teenagers. This does not mean that emotional reactivity was not part of the family system when the children were younger. Teens excel at dramatizing problems. We all have images of a sullen teen who will not communicate or the teen that is acting out and getting into trouble. Teenagers have the capacity to bring these family problems to light in a very dramatic manner.

The emotional reactivity that was learned in childhood persists far into adulthood. Adult children experience this when they go home to visit their parents. After a few days the old patterns in the nuclear family begin re-asserting themselves. The adult child starts to feel like a small child again, even though he or she may be forty years old, reverting back to their vulnerable childhood role. The parents also regress and the atmosphere between the adult child and the parent becomes emotionally raw and very trying for both parties. This difficulty in dealing with emotional reactivity leads some adult children to long-term conflictual or caretaking relationships with their parents.

Others become avoidant and try to restrict visits to their parents to a few days. Some adult children go to the extreme of moving across country to reduce contact. Recognizing the emotional reactivity induced by contact with parents is a very healing exercise.

Having a parent express emotions in a reactive way is very distressing to children. Children are highly vulnerable when distressed because they have such few coping skills. Time spent in emotionally reactive situations while growing up leads to trauma. Children become deeply conditioned by their parents' lack of ability to deal with their ER, and they pass what they have learned down to their own children, who in turn pass it on to their children. The "disease" of emotional reactivity continues and spreads in this way.

Consequences of Emotional Reactivity

There are numerous consequences to ER. On a personal level it may affect us in many ways. It may sabotage our interactions with others. It may contribute to feelings of low self-esteem and erode self-confidence. It tends to drive others away and makes us feel isolated. It may be a career buster—those who are highly reactive come to the attention of those they work for in a negative way. Having difficulty interpersonally is one of the major contributing factors to job loss.

We have learned that emotional reactivity is very destructive among families, creating alienation and becoming a wedge that pushes family members apart. We may remember times growing up when we experienced a family member getting lost in his or her emotions, and the memories of these events are not very pleasant. ER sabotages efforts to be good parents and contributes to dysfunction and abuse in families as no other problem can.

Outside family relationships, ER is just as destructive. The most significant reason that people have difficulty forming long-lasting relationships is that their high levels of emotional reactivity get in the way. They are full of turmoil and unpleasant to be around. The disruption in communication and the negative energy their emotions cause make it difficult for them to resolve problems realistically. Their tempers provide the "straw that breaks the camel's back" in their dealings with friends and co-workers. Having the skills to handle ER is a must for any happy relationship.

In the larger society, emotional reactivity is very damaging. Not only does it exacerbate various medical conditions, but it is also a major trigger of relapse in addictions and may lead individuals to be socially isolated from caring forces that encourage good health and a sense of belonging. It may even lead to crimes, particularly crimes of passion, and is a significant factor in political disputes and wars. The image on television in 1960 of an emotionally reactive Nikita Kruschev, banging his shoe on the table at the United Nations after previously stating "We will bury you," contributed to fueling fear and distrust in the Cold War. Most of the families of dictators were very emotionally reactive and abusive. The tyrant ends up playing out this dysfunction on the world stage, where political power can make thousands suffer.

You may want to think about your own experiences with emotional reactivity—either being the victim of someone else's ER or an experience when you were expressing your own. Consider the consequences to yourself and others in those situations.

Emotional Reactivity is Common to Us All

How prevalent is emotional reactivity? It seems to be universal. We all have an autonomic nervous system and a need to manage our emotional reactions. Murray Bowen saw emotional reactivity on a continuum. Some families, couples, or individuals are very emotionally reactive; others are less emotionally reactive. Everyone is susceptible to ER at various moments in their lives, especially when we are stressed.

Emotional reactivity is not a psychological diagnosis. You don't have to have a mental illness to display it. However, some individuals with mental illness do have a more difficult time handling their emotions, and certain conditions exacerbate the problem. Those with anger issues, personality disorders, post-traumatic stress syndrome and other disorders are high on the emotional reactivity scale. Those who are high in emotional reactivity or who have a difficult time learning skills out of a book may benefit from using the principles presented here with the help of a therapist. It is highly satisfying and empowering to overcome ER and to realize that others have less power to push our buttons.

CHAPTER KEY POINTS

- To master our emotions we need to manage our emotional reactivity.

- Emotional reactivity occurs when the fight-or-flight reaction is triggered.

- There are three habitual modes of emotional reactivity: conflict, avoidance, and caretaking.

- Emotional reactivity is different from the healthy expression of emotions.

- Emotional reactivity is "contagious" and can affect the whole family.

- Emotional reactivity is common to us all and is destructive to ourselves and our children.

EXERCISES

1. Take some time to remember when you have been emotionally reactive. Remember whom you reacted to and what the
   situation was. Does this situation still push your buttons?
   Have you made some progress in not reacting so much in the
   situation? If you made progress, how did this occur?

2. Are there situations that you avoid because of fears of being
   emotionally reactive? Are there, perhaps, people that you
   avoid or don't like to talk to because they push your buttons?

3. Is there a difficult person that you interact with who pushes
   your buttons? How does this person push your buttons?
   What do they do or say that "gets your goat?" Consider your
   relationships with other people who may stimulate emotions
   in you besides anger, such as guilt, shame, hurt, fear, or other
   vulnerable emotions.

4. Are you a caretaker? Do you feel anxious when others around
   you are unhappy? Do you worry more often than your peers
   about those you love? Do you give and give to others but feel
   you do not get much back? Do you feel resentful about this?

CHAPTER 2

Step 1: Taking Responsibility and Setting Good Boundaries

The devil made me do it.

FOLK SAYING

Stop Blaming the Environment

For some people this first step can be the most difficult. We need to accept that we participate in the creation and maintenance of emotional reactivity if we hope to change it. This is often met with resistance because the tendency to externalize is deeply ingrained in human culture. It is particularly easy to blame others or the environment for our emotional reactivity. Not taking responsibility for our emotions compromises our ability to control our reactions. It is essential to realize that ER takes place within us. Another person or the environment may be a trigger, but not the cause of our emotional reactivity.

Joe and Carol came into treatment because of marital problems. Carol was concerned about Joe's out-of-control spending, but their attempts to discuss the issue would trigger angry arguments. They focused on changing each other, rather than focusing on changing themselves. Neither was willing to take responsibility for their poor behavior or communication. Carol complained about Joe's spending and lack of responsibility, and Joe complained about Carol's nagging and verbal abusiveness. They were caught in a stalemate—neither one willing to change or admit a mistake until their spouse did. They each feared that admitting they were wrong would give their spouse the upper hand. Only when they accepted responsibility for their own behavior and communication could they resolve their problems.

Barry and Kathy were at an impasse. Kathy complained to Barry about not picking up his things, and the disorder in which he kept his office, the garage, and any other room he visited. Kathy began to feel like Barry's mother and did not want to pick up after him. Barry felt like Kathy was trying to change him. His argument was that Kathy knew that he was not a tidy person when she married him, and it was unfair that she wanted him to be different now. Each thought the other person was being stubborn, and neither of them saw a need to change themselves. Their discussions about this issue were heated and never moved in the direction of a solution. Because they both were unwilling to take responsibility for their emotional reactivity, they were at an impasse and could not resolve their problem together. Once this couple identified and accepted their actions and reactions, they began to change their dialogue for the better. Their communication became less accusatory, and they became calm enough to work on a solution to their problems. The first step was to stop trying to change the other person and to begin working on themselves.

Reducing the intensity of emotional reactivity allowed this couple to gain the clarity of mind to explore their underlying problems. Barry was confused about what Kathy was asking him to do. He took it as an issue of personal integrity, feeling that Kathy was trying to change who he was as a person. It was important for him to recognize the difference between changing his behavior and changing his essential self. In therapy we explored the many times he had changed his behavior and this had not changed who he was. Barry was a soccer player. To learn a new play or technique, he willingly changed his behavior without feeling a threat to his integrity or changing himself as a person. Integrity issues are about important concerns in our lives, not about bad habits, such as sloppiness. Standing up for important issues in our lives <u>is</u> a matter of integrity. Many people are confused about this issue. They think that when somebody else asks them to change their behavior, that this is an assault on their integrity. It is not.

This made sense to Barry and after thinking about it, he was mystified why he responded so defensively to Kathy's request for neatness. Barry felt the pressure of Kathy's request on the emotional level. This topic over the years had become an emotionally reactive one. He had begun responding more to Kathy's emotions when she asked him to pick up after himself than to her words, and Kathy was no longer calm when she made these requests.

Kathy needed to be realistic about her request. Barry was 31 years old and had been sloppy for a lifetime. The likelihood of his immediately becoming neat was not high. Unconscious behavior patterns are difficult to change because they are done automatically and with little awareness. When Kathy understood how difficult it would be for Barry to change this habit, she eased up on her demand. On the emotional level she saw that she had been taking Barry's lack of neatness personally. She thought that if he loved her he would change. Seeing how her view of the situation contributed to her ER helped her relax and not hand all the responsibility for her upset to Barry. Kathy's greater acceptance of this issue helped Barry, because now Kathy could make her requests more calmly and she no longer appeared to him to be controlling.

Once they both decided to take responsibility for each of their contributions to the problem, their emotional reactivity diminished to reasonable levels. When their ER was out of the way, they quickly began to find solutions to their problems. The reasonable parts of their minds could now solve the problem without getting emotionally sidetracked. Barry made a commitment to work on his sloppiness, and quickly began to improve in this area. Kathy agreed to support him in this. She learned how to remind him in a more gentle manner when he forgot to put something away and agreed not to remind him too often, so Barry would not feel picked on.

We Cannot Change Others, Only Ourselves

It is odd that we externalize and focus so much on changing others, when it is actually an impossible task. People can only change themselves. If we look at the order of how easily things can be changed in our lives, we find that external objects are the easiest to change. We can change the look of a lawn by mowing it and picking up the fallen leaves, or we can change a glass by breaking it. These are relatively easy things to do. At the opposite extreme is changing others. This is impossible; we cannot do it. Therapists know this, too. The best that they can do is create an environment that will encourage clients to change themselves. Midway between changing things (possible), and changing others (impossible) is changing ourselves. It is realistic to believe that change is possible for us as long as we have the motivation, the courage and the proper tools. It is not realistic to focus on changing others.

Externalizing is the act of blaming our problems on the environment or on others. It puts us in a position of attempting to change what we cannot change rather than what we can. This stance leads us to feel victimized. Blaming the outside world gives responsibility for our emotional problems to others, but it is essential that we take responsibility for the part of the problem that is ours. To feel like a victim when we are not undercuts our power. Seeing ourselves as victims increases our emotional reactivity.

Two common manifestations of feeling like a victim are resentment and self-pity—attitudes that lead to emotional reactivity. When we hold a resentment, we believe that our problems stem from what others have done to us. With self-pity our object of resentment is more generalized. We feel fate or life in general has let us down. Both attitudes are dead ends. They make it impossible for us to feel empowered and to make the changes in our lives that will make us feel happier.

Why We Externalize

Externalization is very pervasive. It is structured into our common speech. We say things like, "He made me angry," or "You're making me feel guilty." We hold others responsible for our feelings and emotions, as if they could reach into our bodies and turn our anger or guilt on and off. These emotions occur within us and we are responsible for them. The most that another person can do is to serve as a trigger for our emotions.

Another reason that we externalize is that we confuse emotional reactivity with natural, instinctive emotions based on reality. For instance if I am walking in the woods and see a bear coming toward me, my natural response will be fear. Because my emotion is based on reality and is not a distortion in any way, the emotion of fear is natural to the situation and not problematic. In this context, it seems natural to say that the bear caused the fear, because if the bear wasn't there, I would not experience fear. With emotional reactivity, our emotions are not based on present reality. They are based on the distortions caused by past events in our lives and our distorted views of the present situation. This problem is inside of us rather than something that is external.

Another reason we externalize is because, for many of us, it is difficult to take responsibility for our behavior. Our behavior may conflict with our self-concept. We may have the false notion that we are never wrong about things, that we are always right morally and intellectually. We may be very defensive about looking at and owning responsibility for our emotional reactivity. Change can be scary because it may confront who we think we are.

For others taking responsibility for their ER may be hard because they are used to blaming *somebody*. If they do not blame others they blame themselves—which is different from taking responsibility for oneself. When we self-blame, we put ourselves down — telling ourselves that we are inferior or bad. Instead of taking responsibility for something specific like a behavior, we blame our whole person. Learning the difference between taking responsibility for one's self versus blaming one's self is an important key to not being defensive. When we take responsibility, we look objectively at ourselves and change our attitudes or behavior as appropriate.

Self-blaming is as common as blaming others. Sometimes these two are connected because blaming others can be a defense against self-blame. John could not understand why he was so critical of his girlfriend Margaret. He repetitively found things wrong with her and expressed his criticisms to her. John decided to examine what came over him in the moments before these instances occurred. He saw that immediately prior to criticizing Margaret, he had feelings of insecurity about himself in some way. To avoid these bad feelings, he changed the focus of his attention to Margaret.

Often people feel they only have these two choices open to them—either to blame others or to blame themselves, because they lack the skills necessary to work on their emotional reactivity in a constructive way. When faced with a choice of either blaming others or blaming themselves, they choose blaming others because it is less immediately painful to them. They resist taking responsibility for their actions to avoid beating themselves up and feeling bad.

This avoidance and difficulty in taking responsibility is caused by confusion between behavior on one level versus the self on another level. A person makes a mistake and feels guilty rather than just seeing it as a mistake and changing it. The mistake, which is just a behavior, is wrongly applied to their sense of self. This creates guilt and shame and is not helpful. By not understanding the difference between behavior and the essential self, there is confusion. In this confusion there seems to be only two choices —to take responsibility and feel guilty or to resist taking responsibility at all. When this confusion is clarified, a person is more capable of taking responsibility for their behavior.

When We Externalize, We Lack Clear Boundaries

With emotional reactivity, the external stimulus is merely a trigger for a process that is internal. We can work most readily on our own reactions, and be very clear about our boundaries in terms of responsibility. Usually setting boundaries includes a combination of changing ourselves as well as holding others accountable for their behavior. We have to be clear about which is which. If John does not return the hammer I lent him, the next time I see him I may become very emotionally reactive and criticize him for being an irresponsible friend. My reactions are a combination of his not returning the hammer, and my experiences from the past. Perhaps others have taken advantage of me. John's behavior triggers this old wound. It would be incorrect for me to give total responsibility for my anger to John's negligence. I carry my past into the situation and this causes me to overreact.

Inquiring into how much I am responsible for my emotional reactions can help me distinguish my boundaries in a situation. Is my reaction realistic considering the other person's behavior? If I am being emotionally reactive, I am clearly not acting realistically. My reaction will be overblown, or I will go to the other extreme and avoid any emotional expression whatsoever. How much do I need to work on myself and how much do I need to hold the other person accountable for their actions? Clear boundaries regarding responsibility will help me resolve these situations.

When we stop the "blame game" we can start attending to what needs to be changed in our lives. Externalization and blaming oneself unnecessarily keep emotional reactivity going. Once we focus on applying the skills necessary to change ourselves, our emotional reactivity no longer remains hidden behind our rationalizations and excuses. Blaming is the first barrier that must fall for a person to progress in containing their emotional reactivity.

Setting Boundaries

Identifying and setting boundaries are important steps in managing emotional reactivity. When we have poor boundaries with our loved ones, relationships can become very painful. We either become too enmeshed with them or we go to the opposite extreme and cut ourselves off emotionally from them. Having one's boundaries confused with another's sets us up to get our buttons pushed, leading to inappropriate behavior. An understanding of boundaries may be key to a person's efforts to be free from reactivity.

When we are close to another person and have poor boundaries, we are susceptible to emotional confusion. Boundary confusion between ourselves and another is deeply upsetting. We feel threatened and our fight-or-flight reaction is triggered. If we are unable to set boundaries consciously, we do it unconsciously by automatically getting angry and lashing out, or by withdrawing. Our only hope in these emotionally confusing situations is to be able to understand the boundary problem and to communicate in a manner that resets our boundaries.

Problems with boundaries and emotional reactivity go hand in hand. There are three basic boundary issues that correspond to the three ways people express their emotional reactivity:

- People who are caretakers or people-pleasers have very diffuse or non-existent boundaries. This creates confusion between themselves and others—*enmeshment.*
- People who are more conflict-oriented intrude into other's space and violate others' boundaries.
- Avoidant people have very rigid boundaries and do not allow others to get close.

We have different kinds of boundaries. Our skin is one type of boundary that protects us from the outside environment. Without our skin to protect us physically, we would die. Our survival instincts help protect us from having this boundary violated. We also have emotional boundaries. Emotional boundaries are much more difficult for us to define. Emotional boundaries are more like the boundaries between neighboring states; they help us define who has responsibility for which side of the boundary line. If there is a fire on the California side of the state boundary, it would be inappropriate for a Nevada fire department to respond to the scene without an invitation from somebody in California. Without knowing our emotional boundaries clearly, and having the ability to set them, we become confused in our personal relationships.

Boundaries may get confused in a couple of ways. Other people can violate our boundaries, or we can violate theirs. Boundaries can be violated physically by criminal activity or violence, such as if someone punches you, rapes you, or steals from you. Emotional violations are more subtle; we may not even notice when they occur, yet they can be as harmful as physical violations. Some examples of boundary violations are:

- Trying to control somebody else, or allowing yourself to be controlled.
- Manipulating somebody else or allowing yourself to be manipulated.
- Taking responsibility for another person's feelings or actions, or trying to give responsibility for your feelings and actions to another person.
- Taking on the responsibilities of another person, or letting another take on your responsibilities.

- Not standing up for yourself and asserting your needs, wants, ideas, and feelings.
- Failing to take responsibility for your communication.

Our feelings are the best indicators of emotional boundary violations. If you are interacting with somebody, and during or afterward you feel confused, angry, upset, annoyed, hurt, obsessed with an issue regarding the other person, or some other uncomfortable feeling, you know that there is a boundary problem. Check your boundaries. Then see if you are in somebody else's space or if they are in yours.

Some tips for setting boundaries:

- Realize that you have no control over other people, places, or things.
- Realize that you are responsible for your own feelings, actions, and duties; other people are responsible for theirs.
- Know you have the right to assert yourself and speak your truth.

Areas That Need Boundary Clarification

These are areas of our lives where we may become confused about our boundaries with others. Use this list as a way to develop an understanding of where you may need to set boundaries in your life. This list works well with the steps for setting boundaries that follows it.

Feelings: You are responsible for your own feelings and emotions. They take place within your body. They are your responsibility to identify, understand, communicate, and work through. Although we may trigger someone else's feelings through our behavior, it is a mistake to take ongoing responsibility for how the person deals with these feelings.

Communication: It is your responsibility to communicate clearly. If you keep secrets or hold back, it creates distance between you and others. It is your responsibility to communicate what you want, feel, need, etc. Others cannot read your mind. Everyone needs to be held accountable for dysfunctional and abusive communications.

Responsibilities: If you take on the responsibilities of another, you will enable them to be irresponsible and you will end up not taking care of yourself. If you let another take on your responsibilities unnecessarily, your self-esteem and confidence will disintegrate over time.

Thoughts: You have the right to think independently and to arrive at your own conclusions based on your own experience. You also have the responsibility to be logical in your thinking and not impose your views on others.

Trauma: If you have past trauma, it is important that you set a boundary by not blaming yourself for the trauma. At the same time, it is your responsibility to find help and support for this difficult issue, so that it does not interfere with your relationships.

Intentions: It is important to be aware of and take responsibility for the intentions behind your acts and your communications, because they will have an impact on your relationships.

Behavior: You are responsible for your behavior and no one else's.

There is no justification for faulty communication or inappropriate behavior.

Control: Are you focusing all your attention on controlling another person—getting that person to believe, feel or do what you want? If so, you are outside of your boundary and are violating the other person.

Assertiveness: Some people have a hard time standing up for themselves and sharing with others what they want, need or feel. Others communicate in an aggressive or inappropriate way. To successfully assert ourselves is to communicate honestly, openly and appropriately for the situation.

These are some of the main areas of boundary confusion Boundaries occur in all of human interaction, so this is only a partial list. Remember to take responsibility for everything on your side of the boundary, and let the other person take responsibility (or hold them accountable) for everything on their side of the boundary. Defining our boundaries is one of the main tasks we have in growing up emotionally. Emotional reactivity and poor boundaries go hand in hand.

Steps for Setting Boundaries

There are a number of steps that make boundary setting easier. By working through these steps, you may gain a clearer understanding of your boundaries and feel more confident in setting them.

1. Notice the feelings you have when you interact with somebody else; feelings give you feedback whenever there is a problem.

Whenever you feel disturbed after or during an interaction, recognize that your boundaries need some maintenance. Stop, breathe, and check your body because this is where our feelings originate.

2. Realize there is a boundary problem of some kind. It is helpful to create an anchoring statement of some kind that kicks in at this point, such as: "I feel uncomfortable with that interaction, I'd better check my boundaries."

3. Imagine a line between yourself and the other person. Everything on this side of the line is yours and your responsibility, everything on the other side of the line is the other person's and is their responsibility.

4. Refer to "Areas that Need Boundary Clarification" above to get hints to clarify the boundaries between both of you. You may do this alone, or if the other person is willing and understands the process, you may do it together.

5. Set your boundaries. This usually entails a combination of both internal work and external communication. For instance, if your spouse calls you a name, an internal boundary that may have to be set is to realize that the name is untrue and that put-downs are abusive. Another part of your internal boundary is to not become emotionally reactive and call a name back.

6. Set the external boundary by communicating clearly to the other person. In this case you may want to tell the other person you will not continue the discussion if they continue to attack your character.

7. Remember the key to having good boundaries is the willingness to take responsibility for everything that happens on your side of the boundary. This includes communicating openly and clearly to the other person. It also means holding others accountable for their behavior or the way they communicate.

Successful Relationships Demand Good Boundaries

To have an intimate relationship that works, it is imperative that one has a good sense of boundaries and can communicate well to others. When we are unable to set boundaries consciously, we end up setting them unconsciously. One way we attempt this is through anger and conflict. It is uncomfortable to lose one's boundary with another person. It can be like losing one's sense of self. To avoid this, a person may have an outburst as a way to deal with the confusion and pain of being enmeshed, thereby pushing the other person away. This creates a temporary breathing space that allows the partners to regroup. It also discharges the tension building between the couple due to poor boundaries. Some couples go through this dance like clockwork. They go for a few weeks in peace until the tension slowly builds and there is an explosion of anger. This routine may be repeated again and again. Unfortunately, this type of emotional reactivity can end up pushing the couple away from each other and destroying the relationship.

Another way couples deal with enmeshment and poor boundaries is for one or both partners to become distant. The distance is an unconscious way to protect ourselves from the pain of poor boundaries. Sometimes both partners embrace this solution and the relationship takes on a detached emotional tone. The two partners lead parallel lives, rarely talking to each other except about practical matters and other "safe" topics. The safety of not being enmeshed is gained at the loss of intimacy and connection.

The third unconscious way to deal with the lack of boundaries is to stay enmeshed but focus on another issue. A couple can triangulate somebody else or some problem into their enmeshed relationship – it may be an addiction, a mental health problem, a problem in a child, or a third person—as in having an affair or a common enemy. By focusing attention on the outside problem, the couple can avoid working on the serious issues between them. Couples who do not like direct conflict in their relationships can unconsciously choose this alternative as a symbolic way to act out their problem. The difficulty is that the couple develops an investment in continuing this third problem. Healing can only come when the couple addresses the underlying boundary issue.

To have a healthy relationship it is necessary to maintain boundaries through good communication. All relationships trigger small hurts and disagreements over time. If we can discuss these without emotional reactivity, then it is possible to heal these hurts as they occur and renew intimacy in the relationship. Otherwise the partners stray farther and farther from each other and a great wall is built over time. By reducing our emotional reactivity, we create a sense of safety in the relationship so that this boundary regulation can be done in an atmosphere of love and respect.

Where Have I Felt This Before?

When we are experiencing emotional reactivity we are projecting the past onto the present. Many times we lose track of this, and we think that our reactions are only due to what is happening in the immediate situation. To appreciate how we carry experiences from our past into the present, ask yourself the question: "Where have I felt this before?" This question can get us in touch with similar feelings that we felt in a previous situation.

Linda was sensitive to her boss, Dennis, giving her feedback about her job. His remarks angered her, and she wondered why he couldn't leave her alone and let her do her job. She blew up at Dennis one day and was reprimanded for this. She worried her anger problem could jeopardize her job. She asked herself why this was happening and where she had felt this feeling before. Linda recalled old feelings she had encountered many times around her controlling ex-husband who was very critical of her and in whose eyes she could do no right. When she realized that her boss had stirred up old feelings associated with her ex-husband, Linda could see that she had brought her own baggage into her relationship with Dennis. This helped her take responsibility for her emotional reactivity and increased her motivation to work on the problem.

Seeing that the other person is emotionally reactive due to some past trauma in her life can help us reduce our own emotional reactivity. Linda explained to Dennis that previous altercations with her controlling ex-husband caused her to react to him so strongly, and this helped Dennis understand Linda better. He felt more compassion for her after she told him about her problem and gained hope that because Linda knew what the underlying problem was and was taking responsibility for it, she would be able to work it through. Fortunately for Linda, her willingness to take responsibility for her emotional reactivity saved her job.

When couples understand why their partner is responding the way they are, their compassion and hope for the relationship increases. The closed context of emotional reactivity opens, allowing both partners to understand the real causes of their own, and the other person's emotional reactivity. Seeing a loved one finally take responsibility for his or her emotional reactivity after many years of hopelessness is a wonderful experience and may serve as an open invitation for the other person to do so, also.

The Serenity Prayer

The Serenity Prayer contains much wisdom and is useful when dealing with problems of externalization and blame.

> *God, grant me the serenity to accept the things I cannot change, the courage to change the things I can, and the wisdom to know the difference. Amen.*

By learning clear boundaries, we learn that what is ours is often changeable. What belongs to others we can never change, only they can. Knowing this is true wisdom.

CHAPTER KEY POINTS

- It is important that we take responsibility for our emotional reactivity as a first step in managing it.

- We must overcome the habit of blaming the environment when we are upset.

- Having good boundaries is essential to the mastery of emotions.

- There are basic areas in our lives that create boundary confusion.

- Seven steps for setting boundaries are described.

- Maintaining healthy boundaries is essential for successful relationships

EXERCISES

1. Can you remember a time in your life when you blamed someone else for your unhappiness or anger? Have you ever had someone do this to you?

2. Is it difficult to admit that you may be wrong? Are you close to someone who cannot admit being wrong?

3. Is it difficult to take responsibility for your behavior without putting yourself down and feeling bad about yourself?

4. Think of a time in your life when you stopped blaming others and instead you took responsibility for your own reactivity. What were the results of this?

5. Are there people in your life whom you always have difficulties with? There is probably some type of boundary problem you are having with that person. Use the above exercises to identify this boundary problem.

6. Do you have a tendency toward one of the three types of boundary problems? Are you a caretaker whose boundaries are enmeshed and unclear? Are you conflict oriented and do you intrude into other people's space? Are you an avoider with rigid boundaries that prevents others from getting close?

7. Rate yourself from one to ten on how well-defined you feel your boundaries are. One is extremely poor and ten indicates perfect boundaries. You may find that this rating varies depending on which relationship you are examining in your life.

CHAPTER 3

Step 2: Developing A Strong Intention

"Our intention creates our reality."

WAYNE DYER

Once a person stops blaming others, then the next step is to develop a strong intention to change. Emotional reactivity is difficult to change because it relies on mechanisms that are not always in our conscious awareness. It takes consistent effort. ER is based on bad habits that we may have been practicing for years. The only way to overcome these old habit patterns is to be aware of them and replace them with healthier responses.

There are two significant variables that determine how quickly and thoroughly a person can transform emotional reactivity into a compassionate response. One is the intensity of the emotional reactivity. The more intense it is, the more difficult it can be to change. We are either more emotionally reactive or we are less emotionally reactive. Fortunately, the intensity of our emotional reactivity is something we can lessen through the techniques presented throughout this book.

The other variable is the level of desire that we have for change, and this is something that we can increase. People have different levels of motivation to work on their emotional reactivity. Those with little desire for change make less progress, and those with a strong desire for change progress more quickly.

The desire for change has to be quite high for us to be successful in changing something as complex as emotional reactivity. Even people with high ER, who may have a history of abuse or abandonment as children, can make rapid progress. It depends on the strength of their desire to change. Others, whose level of emotional reactivity is low and whose motivation is also low may make little progress. To build their desire for change, they have to understand that emotional reactivity is damaging to their relationships. As their motivation increases, so does progress in this area.

The Negative Consequences of Emotional Reactivity

One of the prime methods of motivating oneself for change is to recognize the negative consequences of a behavior. Emotional reactivity has many negative consequences in our lives. As described in the last chapter it is very easy for people to blame others for their emotional reactivity without taking a good look at themselves. To develop a strong intention to change, we must see how ER affects our lives. Following is a list of negative consequences of emotional reactivity. It is helpful to review this list and see how they apply to your situation.

- **Unsuccessful relationships**. Emotional reactivity is a destructive force in our personal relationships. It tears apart marriages and families.
- **Volatile relationships**. If you have a high level of emotional reactivity, you may attract another person who has the same level of ER. People with lower reactivity usually are not attracted to people with high ER.
- **Stress**. Emotional reactivity is very hard on the body. It activates the fight-or-flight response. This is debilitating to the body if it persists or occurs often.
- **Health**. Because of the destructive nature of this stressful reaction, it can be dangerous to our health.
- **Suffering**. When we are emotionally reactive we suffer pain that, in turn, affects the people around us.
- **Diminished success in life**. Emotionally reactive people get fired more often, get fewer promotions, and have less success in all areas of their lives.
- **Destruction of the family unit**. ER is a major contributing factor to separation and divorce. It creates a painful environment for children to be around. Children learn to be emotionally reactive from their caretakers.

The list above helps in understanding the importance of changing emotional reactivity. Review your history to see how your emotional reactivity has affected you and the lives of your loved ones. This exercise is not to create guilt. Self-punishment and self-blame for past mistakes does not help, and may decrease self-esteem, making it more difficult to change. Recognizing the negative consequences of ER is an important step in increasing our desire for change.

It has been said that when we want something wholeheartedly, we will find a way to obtain it. This is true when seeking a realistic goal for ourselves. A problem occurs when there is ambivalence. We may have hidden reasons why we do not reach our goals. There may be fears of actually having what we seek, worries about how much work it would be to get it, or a belief that we don't deserve what we are seeking. Here is an exercise that you can use to explore the wholeheartedness of your desire for anything that you want. I call it The List. Then we will see an example of how this is used for overcoming emotional reactivity.

The List

Step One: Name the desire. What is your goal?

Step Two: List the positive reasons that you want this thing. What will it do for you?

Step Three: What are the negative beliefs that could hold you back? Think of every negative reason why you cannot get it, or fears of what would happen if you did get it. Is there any belief that you don't deserve it or can't attain it?

Step Four: Reframe. Explore your hesitations and revise them so that they are not negative, distorted or exaggerated. Are these things really true? What is the evidence that they are true?

Here is an example of one person using The List to explore his resistance to working on his emotional reactivity.

John's List.

Step One: Name the desire. I would like to transform my emotional reactivity and have a better relationship with my wife, Sue.

Step Two: Listing the positives if you get your desire. I would be happier. She would be happier. We would get along better. The kids wouldn't get so upset seeing us arguing.

Step Three: What are the negative beliefs that hold you back. I can't do it. I am afraid it takes too much effort. I have a fiery temper. I don't want to give that up. That is part of me.

Step Four: Reframe.

I can't do it. How do I know this to be true? I have never really tried to change it, so to assume that I can't do it is false. A more truthful way to put this is "This looks hard and I am afraid that I will fail, but I may succeed also."

I am afraid it takes too much effort. Yes, it may take a lot of effort, but that is O.K. The effort is worth it for my family and me to be happier. It probably takes more out of me to be emotionally reactive.

59

I have a fiery temper. I don't want to give that up. It is part of me. It is true that I have a fiery temper. I don't know if it will always be true. It may be possible to change if I learn to express myself in a more constructive manner. I don't want to give it up because it is part of my identity. However, I have changed many things about myself in the past, and these changes made my life better. It may be an illusion that if I gave this up, I would lose a big part of myself. Maybe, I don't have to give up my fiery nature, I just need to make it work better for me.

Do this exercise to ferret out any unknown negatives you may have about transforming your emotional reactivity. Consider using this exercise for anything you want in your life that seems to be eluding you.

A Deep Desire Can Cut Through the Deepest Unconsciousness

When I was ten years old my uncle Stan would come and pick me up on a Saturday morning to go fishing with him. I loved to fish. It was a particular treat for me to go fishing with my uncle because he was an excellent fisherman and took me to the best fishing places. The only problem was that Uncle Stan wanted to pick me up at six o'clock in the morning and I usually slept until ten on Saturday. My parents did not want to get up that early on Saturday morning to wake me up either.

I borrowed my parent's alarm clock and set it for 5:30 AM. I was so excited about fishing, however, that I woke up before the alarm rang. This continued to happen before every fishing trip. It was not uncommon for me to wake up a few minutes before the alarm would ring. My desire to go fishing was so strong that it was able to wake me up out of a deep sleep. The strong intention to go fishing overcame my deeply ingrained habit of sleeping late.

If you are determined to transform your emotional reactivity, you will find that a strong desire will wake you up at the most needed times. This will be especially helpful in the midst of the strong emotions that are characteristic of ER. It is quite amazing how this can happen. Build a strong intention and see how well it works in waking you up at the most important moments of emotional reactivity. If you become emotionally reactive and say something or do something destructive, don't let it get you down. Use it as fuel to build your resolve to change this in yourself. Although emotional reactivity can be a very strong force in us, it cannot stand up to a strong, consistent intention to change it.

Therapy Can Help In Keeping Your Motivation High

Many individuals, couples, and families use the services of a psychotherapist to keep their motivation high. Going to a therapist regularly is a steady reminder of the behaviors that need to be changed to work through emotional reactivity. Unless you have a serious psychological disorder, having consistent, strong motivation along with the steps presented in this book is all that is needed to overcome this difficult problem. Emotional reactivity will not be mastered all at once. Keep chipping away at it and you will find success.

CHAPTER KEY POINTS

- We must develop a strong intention to be able to overcome something as challenging as emotional reactivity.

- It is helpful to be aware of the negative consequences of emotional reactivity to build the motivation necessary to overcome it.

- A technique called The List can be used to build motivation buy addressing our fears, and the potential outcome of our behaviors.

EXERCISES

To further your effort to develop a strong intention, try using The List exercise in this chapter with the goal of transforming your emotional reactivity. Here is The List:

1. Name the desire. What is your goal?
2. List the reasons you want to change your emotional reactivity. Consider the negative consequences of your emotional reactivity. Consider your desire to have more healthy relationships.
3. List all the negative beliefs you have about trying to change your emotional reactivity. Consider some of the following:
   - It will take too much energy.
   - I won't be able to do it.
   - I believe that my life would be somehow worse if I didn't have my ER.
4. Reframe each of these hesitations by questioning their validity.

CHAPTER 4

Step 3: Stopping Dysfunctional Behavior

*"Remember not only to say the right thing in the right place,
but far more difficult still, to leave unsaid the wrong
thing at the tempting moment."*

BENJAMIN FRANKLIN

Old Behaviors Reinforce Emotional Reactivity

The most destructive component of emotional reactivity is behavior. When we are upset, our actions may go far beyond what is normal for us. If our usual reaction is aggression, we may do something regrettable. Our legal system understands that when people are upset, they may behave in ways that are not normal for them. Consequently, there is a lesser penalty for manslaughter than there is for pre-meditated murder. Countless destructive behaviors can occur when we are emotionally reactive, and they have the potential to create huge problems for us. Besides aggression, other dysfunctional behaviors include such things as addiction relapse, passive-aggressive behaviors, avoidance, and communicating something that we later regret.

These behaviors are often assimilated at an early age and thus become inflexible and habitual. Usually, they are accompanied by a deep belief that this behavior must be continued or something terrible will happen. Aggressive behavior can serve as a distraction from deeper feelings of vulnerability that have been covered up for years. This helps explain the compulsivity of the behaviors that are part of ER.

Acting out reinforces emotional reactivity. The two most common behavioral responses are fight or flight, both of which are instinctive and easily conditioned reactions. Both also provide the reward of less anxiety and tension. Once a person gets angry and blows-up, he or she feels better from letting off steam. Similarly, by choosing to avoid and withdraw, the person immediately reduces anxiety by removing himself from the triggering situation.

Change the Behavior First

When we act out, we express our emotional reactivity in a manner that is often contagious to others. Our negative behavior may stimulate others' emotional reactivity, making it more likely that they will respond with negative behavior. This negative feedback loop between two people can lead to such high arousal that no positive communication is allowed to take place.

Aggressive behaviors and negative reactions can be so distracting that it seems impossible to think clearly or to choose alternative behaviors. They leave no room for anything else to occur. If we can slow things down and examine the situation, we can make better decisions and choose more positive ways of behaving.

The ability to change behavior is influenced by many factors, including motivation, ability, and the perception that new behaviors are available. Emotional reactivity deals with emotional issues from the past, making the behavior much harder to change. A person may know better, be reasonably motivated, and have the capability of changing their behavior in less emotionally reactive situations. However, the more upset they become, the more difficult it is to control their behavior. That is because these ingrained behaviors are deeply habitual and can be as difficult a challenge to change as addiction. It takes significant effort to overcome emotional reactivity, but with persistent effort this can be changed.

The importance of stopping negative behavior as a prerequisite for emotional healing has long been recognized in psychotherapy. There was a time when addicts sought psychotherapy, but did not stop using alcohol or drugs. This led to very little success for talk therapies in treating addiction, because therapists only addressed the "underlying problems" without addressing the addictive behavior. The advent of Alcoholics Anonymous and other twelve-step groups rectified this imbalance by placing the focus back on the behavior — the use of drugs and alcohol. Once an alcoholic stopped drinking, he found himself in a position to make significant changes in other areas of his life. Sobriety also opened the way to emotional healing.

Some people who lose a family member turn to alcohol or drugs. Even though they may express their sadness about their loss many times in a state of drunkenness, they do not seem to be able to move through their grief. However, when they enter recovery and recall their loss while sober, many respond as if the person died yesterday. It's as if their grief was put on hold as long as they were involved in addictive behaviors. Only after they stop drinking are they able to truly experience their grief and move through it.

The behaviors that occur when we are emotionally reactive are not only dysfunctional, they make it impossible to change on an emotional level. If we are to change an emotional issue from the past, we need to work on all three components of that emotional issue. We need to experience the feelings involved completely, and question the distorted thinking that supports the emotional reactivity. Our dysfunctional behaviors need to change, also. Acting out inhibits the greater healing process.

Emotional Reactivity Wreaks Havoc in Our Lives

The first step in changing any difficult behavior is to examine it objectively and determine if it is harmful. This may be harder than it seems. Many times we do not want to look at our troublesome behaviors. We minimize the damage done by our destructive behaviors or communication, and make excuses for ourselves, "Well, he shouldn't have made me so angry;"or"I didn't get enough sleep the night before." Negative behaviors are hard to admit because we may feel shame or guilt about them if we look too closely. We may also feel hopeless in changing them.

A cost-benefit analysis can be helpful to apply to any behavior that we express when emotionally reactive. Ask yourself what benefits you derive from your behavior and contrast that to its negative consequences. Make a list detailing the negative consequences of continuing that behavior and of the positive rewards of giving up the behavior. By comparing the lists, it becomes apparent how severe the costs are of negative behavior and how much life would improve if we changed the behavior. A cost-benefit analysis can motivate us to change and help us look at our behaviors more objectively without excuses or rationalizations.

A major roadblock to behavior change is the tendency to justify. It is easy to find reasons for negative behavior, usually by placing blame on another person's behavior. "I called her a name, because she called me one." "He deserves to be put down, he's such a jerk." But there is never good justification for dysfunctional behavior or bad communication. The tendency to justify may be deep-seated and difficult to admit, particularly while in the midst of strong emotion. We must be vigilant so we do not justify bad behavior.

It is important to make the distinction between behavior that is connected to emotional reactivity and the natural expression of emotions. Dysfunctional behaviors need to be changed. Natural expressions of emotions should be left alone. They are not voluntary behaviors. For instance, when we are upset, we may cry, or if we are overjoyed we may laugh and clap our hands together. These are natural expressions of emotion and are not dysfunctional. Suppressing or stopping them could lead to suppression of our emotions and cause difficulties for us.

The Three Most Common Types of Behavior to Change

It is helpful to be aware of the three basic behavior patterns of the fight-or-flight response in regard to emotionally reactive behaviors: conflict, avoidance, and caretaking. We must become aware of a behavior before it can be changed. Those with conflictual behaviors may wish to change other people, but this leads to violating others' boundaries. Sometimes the only way to sense if we are being intrusive to others is to be aware of the obsessiveness we experience in our determination to change somebody. Although the emotionally reactive person may feel justified in their actions, conflictual behaviors can be aggressive and hurtful,.

Avoidant behaviors are fueled by strong feelings of wanting to shut down and escape from an impending conflict. Sometimes it is difficult to acknowledge avoidant behaviors because they are often pre-emptive. We avoid facing the situation of high arousal before it occurs, and we develop a justification for the avoidance. Sometimes the only clue we have of this avoidance is that we are being motivated by fear and anxiety rather than wisdom.

Caretaking behaviors may also be pre-emptive and associated

with emotional reactivity. Caretaking is different than true caring because caretakers avoid being honest with others and are afraid to confront them when they are hurtful or self-destructive. They want to avoid conflict at any cost by focusing only on how to please the other person, or they overly fear for the safety of the other person. People-pleasers go to extremes to avoid conflict by anticipating when others might get upset and by soothing them before that can happen. They tell themselves they are "just being loving," and they make rationalizations for focusing more on others at the expense of themselves. Caretakers do not consider their own needs and have trouble setting limits with others.

There are other reactive behaviors that are not included in the categories above. Here are some examples: A child says something to make a parent feel guilty to manipulate the parent into giving the child something he wants. A teenage boy shames a peer to increase his own status with his peer group and lower the status of his peer. There are many ways of manipulating others by using the emotional level of communication.

Stopping Poor Communication

For most people, problematic behavior is not physical violence—it is poor communication. Faulty communication is hurtful to others and provokes other's emotional reactivity. People are more aware of their poor behavior than their poor communication. Missteps in communication are more subtle and harder to define, while

71

bad behavior may be more apparent to us. It is helpful to specify these common, negative communications so they may be clarified and stopped. It is more effective to eliminate faulty ways of communicating first and then to learn positive communication skills. Eliminating the faulty communicators is a big step in reducing emotional reactivity, since each faulty communication is so potent in triggering ER in the other person. Once emotional reactivity is decreased, a couple or family is more open to learning and practicing healthy communication skills.

Below is a list of the most common faulty communications. Review the list and ask yourself if you communicate in any of these ways. Do not be disappointed if you identify with many of them, because everyone uses them at some time in their lives. These methods of communicating are destructive and encourage hurt, defensiveness and resentment. By identifying and eliminating them, we can open the way to healthy communication and reduce emotional reactivity.

1. **Discounting:** We undermine another's feelings, point of view, or what they find important. "How could you feel that?" or "I can't believe you like country music," discounts their feelings. Rolling your eyes in response is also hurtful.

2. **Put downs, name calling, and labeling**: We make a personal attack on someone's character rather than focus on the other's behavior. "You're just lazy." "You can't do anything right." Calling names is not appropriate unless the name is both affectionate and welcomed by the person.

3. **Sarcasm:** This is a put down using voice tone, exaggeration, etc.

4. **Silence as punishment:** We manipulate others by not talking to them and by withdrawing.

5. **Leaving the scene:** We abandon communication with others, without excusing ourselves or without making an appointment time in the future to talk about the problem.

6. **Bringing up past history:** We rub the other person's nose in her past deeds. We trigger the other person to feel bad about themselves. Very few people are strong enough to hear more than one negative at a time. The only time it is appropriate to bring up another person's past history is when we have permission from them and there is a spirit of learning from these past events.

7. **Needing to be right and not being able to say we're sorry:** We do not take responsibility for our actions. Past conflicts become difficult to resolve.

8. **Denial of feelings:** We tell others we are not angry, upset, or hurt, when we obviously are.

9. **Making assumptions:** We assume what another's intentions, feelings or thoughts are. We communicate these assumptions as if they were facts without checking them out.

10. **Defensiveness:** Instead of listening and responding to criticism, we deny or counterattack.

11. **Martyrdom:** We blame our misery on somebody else or suffer in silence. We play the victim.

12. **Not listening:** We don't focus on what the other is saying. We interrupt, finish their sentences, think about our own counter-arguments, or we ignore them by spacing out.

13. **Cross complaining:** We respond to a complaint by bringing up another complaint in retaliation.

14. **Fixing the other:** We rush toward giving the other person solutions rather than listening to them.

15. **Arguing over the facts:** We do not focus on the underlying feelings and concerns that are the basis for the disagreement.

16. **Holding back:** We don't share how we are feeling or what we really want. This creates distance in our relationships.

17. **Staying in the negative:** We express our resentment and criticism, but do not express our love, appreciation, or give compliments.

18. **Using "always" or "never":** When describing other people's behavior, there are usually many exceptions.

19. **Justifying:** We justify our abusive behavior or hurtful communication. We make excuses rather than take responsibility. There is no justification for hurtful actions and poor communication.

20. **Badgering:** We repeat and bring up the same things over and over again, or we do not let another person excuse themselves from an argument. Neither person has the opportunity to calm down and collect themselves.

21. **Intimidation:** We use anger and a loud tone of voice to get our way with others.

22. **"You" language:** We focus our discussion on the other person, rather than talk about our own feelings and concerns.

23. **Not telling the whole truth about our feelings:** We express our anger, but not the other more vulnerable emotions that accompany the anger, such as hurt, fear, shame, etc. Or conversely, we only display our positive feelings—never confronting more painful issues with the other person.

24. **Not being specific:** We do not give others feedback about specific behaviors that are difficult for us. The other person remains confused about what change is needed, what they are doing that upsets us, or about what we want or need.

25. **Mind reading:** We expect the other to know what we want, feel, think, or need without us telling them. We feel angry and resentful when they do not read our minds.

This list specifies the most common ways we communicate poorly to others. It is not only helpful in our efforts to stop these behaviors in ourselves, but it also alerts us to faulty communications in others, thereby making it possible to provide feedback so that they may understand and change their behavior, if so inclined. If individuals in a relationship hold each other accountable for faulty communication and embrace eliminating poor communication together, they can make great strides to "clean up" their communication and reduce emotional reactivity. Even if one person in a relationship stops using this damaging style of speaking, it will diminish ER and help the relationship. By referring to the list immediately after an argument, one may discover exactly what triggered the emotional reactivity.

Basic Communication Skills

Of course we need to replace our poor communication with positive skills. The following is a summary of basic communication skills that can be helpful for that purpose:

1. **Listening:** This is one of the most important skills in communication. The capacity to pay attention to others and listen to them is something that can be practiced and improved over time. Passive listening is when we listen but do not say anything. Active listening lets the other person know we hear them by nodding our head or reflecting back to them what they have told us.

2. **Give and take:** Good conversation is a balance between talking and listening. If you find yourself doing too much of one or the other, you could be out of balance. If we say nothing or we talk all the time, this could ultimately drive others away.

3. **Be specific:** It is important to be specific about what we want, what behaviors we would like other people to change, or what needs to be done.

4. **Ask for what you want:** You have the right to ask, and the other person has the right to say "yes" or "no" to your request. If you do not ask you may not receive what you need.

5. **Use a normal tone:** Do not speak too softly or too loudly.

6. **Request positively** what you want, rather than criticize. It is much more effective to ask your spouse nicely to give you a

foot massage, than to criticize him for not giving you enough of them.

7. **Complain about the behavior rather than criticize the person.** If you have a complaint, make sure you stick to their behavior rather than criticize the person. "You said you would mow the lawn last week and it never got done. Could you do it this weekend?" is much better than a criticism such as: "Not doing the lawn again this week just shows how lazy you are."

8. **Be assertive** rather than passive or aggressive. This means stating what you want, think, need, or feel in an appropriate way.

9. **Gentle Repetition:** It is difficult for many people to hear feedback about their behavior because of sensitivity to criticism. It also is difficult for a person to change a long-standing behavior. Gentle reminders can be helpful and more effective than harsh confrontation.

10. **Ask for permission to give feedback:** A simple question can open the gates of receptivity in another person. The question is, "May I give you some feedback?" Once the person says "yes," then they are much more receptive to your comments than if they do not give you permission.

11. **Use this helpful formula for giving another person feedback about something that bothers you:**
    When you... (Specify the behavior that is affecting you negatively.)
    I feel... (Tell them exactly how you feel—angry, upset, hurt, sad, disappointed, etc.)

Could you please... (Request a specific behavior change.)
In business relationships this can be shortened to a simple,
"I would appreciate it if you did not (call me names, keep
badgering me about that) anymore." Again it is important
to be specific about the behavior you want changed. Many
individuals have difficulty changing their behavior, so be
prepared to repeat your request.

Negative behaviors can be difficult to change. It is important for a
person to have an attitude of determination and a belief that they can
change in order to overcome these behaviors. Working on the other
two components of emotional reactivity — the feeling component
and the distortions in thinking—will reinforce the efforts made to
change negative behavior.

Facing Issues and Wisely Ignoring

There are two extremes of behavior that stimulate emotional reactivity, and a balance must be struck between them. Marriages often fail
because either the issues that need to be addressed in the relationship
are avoided, or they are brought up too much.

John had a difficult time talking about difficulties in his marriage to
Vickie. He felt that he was in over his head in dealing with emotional
issues because Vickie was much more adept at dealing with feelings
and talking about them. John did not like to bring things up because
he always felt like he lost when he did, so he avoided confrontation

altogether. When Vickie mentioned something that needed to be resolved, John left the room. If Vickie was particularly insistent, John shut down. This constant avoidance of issues made it impossible for this couple to resolve any of their difficulties. John did not have the skills to negotiate a relationship and the marriage eventually ended. His avoidance of issues was a prescription for disaster. There is no way to work out problems if they can't be discussed.

Becca was very attracted to psychotherapy and the insights she gained from it. Through her reading she had learned a great deal about herself. She felt it was important to be honest and straightforward about her feelings. She tried to apply this in her marriage to her husband Tim by bringing up issues daily that they needed to work on. The couple set up appointments in the evenings to discuss the communication problems they were having. Becca wanted Tim to share more with her and not be evasive. But this daily attempt at communication began to wear heavily on the marriage. Their problems were relatively minor, yet these problems became the topic of conversation in almost all of their free time together. Eventually the couple became emotionally reactive and argumentative. They had few peaceful, loving times with each other. The marriage began to falter as they began to irritate each other more and more. In Becca's zeal to fix the marriage, and make it more intimate, she was destroying it. There was too much focus on the negative and not enough on what was right in their relationship. The problem orientation that they adopted did not reflect the actual level of difficulty in the relationship.

Wisely ignoring is to know when to ignore an issue and when to address it. There is a balance that should reflect the seriousness of problems in a relationship. If there is domestic abuse or addiction, these problems are so pervasive that it would be unrealistic to ignore them. When the problems are minor, they need to be brought up, but only at the proper time and not all the time. Before dinner, when both spouses have low blood sugar, or when a partner is stressed out, may not be the best time to discuss an issue. It may be better addressed at another time Ignoring issues or overworking them are potential triggers of emotional reactivity.

Stopping one's emotionally reactive behavior can bring up strong feelings. We may feel more vulnerable because our behavior has served as one of our defenses when we are upset. Letting go of automatic behavior can bring us face to face with feelings that we fear. For instance, we may have used anger as a way to distract us from underlying pain. When we stop our negative behavior we need to be able to deal with any strong feelings that may arise, which is the focus of the next chapter.

CHAPTER KEY POINTS

- It is imperative that we stop the destructive behaviors triggered by emotional reactivity.

- Examples of faulty communication are described as well as good communication skills.

- Sometimes it is important to wisely ignore others' provocations, bad habits, and emotional reactivity.

EXERCISES

1. What style of behavior do you prefer? Are you a conflict-oriented, avoidant or caretaking type? What behavior do you automatically use when you are emotionally reactive? What behavior do you use to avoid conflict or other strong emotions?

2. Review the list of faulty communicators. Which ones have you used in the past? Which ones do you still use? Do you know people that use these faulty communicators with you? Which ones do they use?

3. Ask a family member, spouse, or good friend to review the list of faulty communications. Ask them to give you feedback about which ones you use.

4. Using the method of giving feedback given in this chapter, imagine how you would respond if someone talked to you in a negative way. Can you use the "When you..., I feel..., Could you please...?" format to hold this person accountable for their faulty communication?

CHAPTER 5

Step 4: Embracing
Our Feelings

*"Emotion is the chief source of all becoming conscious.
There can be no transforming of darkness into light and
of apathy into movement without emotion."*

C.G. JUNG

Feeling an Emotion

In order to change the difficult behaviors that occur when we are emotionally reactive it is necessary to replace them with new and more functional behaviors. This may result in an increased awareness of our feelings. Habitual behaviors serve to take our attention away from underlying feelings that seem overwhelming. When these behaviors stop, the smoke clears and the underlying feelings become more apparent to us.

Coping with feelings demands skills that are radically different from the skills described in the last chapter for dealing with behavior. To handle the feeling component of an emotion, take the opposite approach. Instead of stopping the feeling, allow it. Instead of changing the feeling to something more positive, embrace it as it is.

The healthy response to feeling is to not change it, move away from it, or distract attention from it. Instead, embrace the feeling with awareness. Feeling is a natural response of our bodies to a situation, or at least to how we perceive that situation. Problems that we have with our emotions lie in distorted perceptions, not in feelings. Feelings demand to be fully felt. If we push the feeling away, we replace it with numbness and repression or with self-destructive actions that distract from feelings. Avoidance of feelings is the source of painful symptoms and defenses. This is why it is so important to embrace feelings, even when we are being emotionally reactive.

Many people run away when confronted with uncomfortable feelings. They are unpleasant; they seem negative. To embrace them is like doing a 180-degree turn. Why embrace unpleasant feelings— like the feelings that accompany emotional reactivity? It is important to understand that they are not destructive. Rather, the behaviors that are used to avoid these feelings are the destructive element. For instance, a person may feel sadness over the loss of a friend, and instead of feeling the sadness will drown his sorrows in drink. In this scenario, drinking is destructive. Embracing the feelings of grief, however, will eventually lead to their transformation.

Over the course of a lifetime we develop numerous, unconscious methods to avoid painful feelings. By embracing our feelings, the compulsion to act these strategies out is short-circuited, and we take the wind out of the sails of defensiveness. If one's tendency is to avoid feelings of hurt by becoming angry, once that hurt is embraced and allowed, then the strategy of avoiding hurt by getting angry has no more purpose. The underlying pain and hurt is faced and transformed.

Painful feelings often become associated with painful events. We believe that if we allow the feelings to arise, we will be vulnerable and hurt again. But the feelings we experience now are not those of past experiences. They are merely changes in our physiology and are not necessarily harmful. What is harmful is running away from our feelings. By embracing painful feelings instead of pushing them away, we can heal.

A feeling is made up of sensations in our bodies as nerve cells become activated. Blood flow changes, adrenaline increases and other chemical changes occur when we are emotional. Feeling is the awareness of these many sensations being stimulated, along with an evaluation of pleasantness, unpleasantness or neutrality. Negative feelings in themselves cannot be horrible or overwhelming, only unpleasant. The true negativity resides in our beliefs and thoughts about them. Understanding this can be a powerful reminder that feelings are okay and are not monsters to be avoided.

Learning to Soothe Ourselves

One analogy we can use is to compare our emotions to the responses of an infant, because infants are highly emotional and have not yet developed the defenses or intellects of adults. They are very sensitive on a feeling level. When an infant is upset and runs to her mother, the mother needs only to hold the infant and attend to her to calm the high emotional arousal of the infant. Being held by a loving caregiver creates a situation in which the original emotion changes, sometimes to its opposite. The child may be laughing and smiling within a few minutes. Feelings require similar attention. We need to soothe ourselves by holding the feeling and staying with it until it changes–until we feel soothed and calmed down.

The ability to soothe our selves emotionally is a principal skill in mastering emotions. We learn this from our caregivers when we are infants. Those unable to soothe themselves may experience distressing emotions for longer periods of time. Often dysfunctional behaviors serve as distractions from these uncomfortable feeling states. By learning to embrace the feeling component of our emotions and to soothe our selves, the impetus for these negative behaviors decreases dramatically. The troublesome behaviors may remain as a habit, but the compulsion to act them out loses much of its power.

It is of primary importance that we change our view of our emotions. We need to stop trying to change them or avoid them, instead, let them come to full awareness. If we can make this discovery — that feelings are our friends and have important information for us — we can build the necessary skills to master our emotions and our reactivity.

Steps for Embracing Our Feelings

1. Move your attention to the feeling rather than away from it.

2. Bring your awareness fully to the feeling without backing away or getting distracted. Stay with the feeling.

3. Explore the feeling. What does it feel like? Are there images that occur to you as you explore the feeling? Note the images but keep your attention on the feeling.

4. Notice the specific parts of your body that are affected by the feeling. Where in your body are you feeling this? See if you can break the feeling down into its component parts. Notice what specific sensations are in your body.

5. Let your breathing relax. Take a deep breath. As you do this, imagine that you are breathing directly into the area where you are feeling the emotion.

6. Be aware if the feeling changes, and notice its energetic quality. Whether the feeling is anger or sadness, it is just energy. Stay with the feeling and see what changes take place.

This exercise should be soothing. If it is not, there may be some fears or memories holding this feeling in place and not allowing it to move.

Sometimes emotions arise like storms that threaten to overwhelm us. We feel as if a catastrophe will sweep over us and carry us away. Comments often made during these intense moments are "I can't stand this," or "I can't bear to feel that way again." Thinking this way leads us to believe that we may never learn to master our response to intense emotion. We frighten ourselves by this misinterpretation of feeling. This fear may become quite pervasive and needs to be questioned deeply. Attending to what is happening in our bodies rather than what we are thinking can be helpful. For instance, with anger we have negative thoughts about who has made us angry, but we also have changes occurring in our bodies. Adrenaline flows, our heart rate increases and our blood pressure rises. Paying attention to these sensations can help us be more realistic and not feel as if our emotions will overwhelm us.

By staying with the feeling and experiencing it in our bodies, we contain it and own it. It does not own us. Knowing that feelings are sensations in our bodies allows us to form a container around them. Awareness is the container that surrounds the emotion and it is larger than the emotion. Awareness contains everything that we are experiencing in the moment: sights, sounds, thoughts, sensations in our bodies. We may be feeling extreme anger in every cell of our bodies, yet our awareness is greater. We can see the trees and the sky, and they have nothing to do with our anger. Instead of seeing anger as a force that sweeps us away, reduce the anger to its true size. Notice how the emotion appears in your body whenever a strong emotion occurs.

As we learn to embrace and experience feeling, a significant transformation takes place—the feelings change. Our feelings have one basic need — to be felt. When we receive this message, it fulfills its task. The feeling may then move to calmness or some other more positive emotion as long as there is no distorted thinking to support its continuance.

Another thing that takes place as we embrace feeling is a change in our deep belief structure. Negative beliefs about experiencing intense feelings fade. We realize that we have embraced the most intense feelings, yet nothing horrible has happened to us, and this helps us break the deep associative ties between these feelings and previous experiences of abuse and distress. We learn that by feeling the feelings, we may soothe ourselves and calm ourselves down. Embracing our feelings now leads to a positive and healing outcome. This is a key method of healing faulty emotional learning that occurs during abusive situations and comes to the surface when we are emotionally reactive.

Numbness and Embracing Feelings

As cited earlier, there are three basic ways of expressing emotional reactivity—through conflict, caretaking and avoidance. All three of these methods avoid feelings to some extent. Let's explore how avoiders can come into greater contact with their emotions.

The avoidant style can be so pervasive for some that it becomes part of their personality style. Because it is difficult for them to experience strong emotions, they avoid them altogether and rarely allow themselves to feel. It may appear that they are not emotionally reactive because they seem calm and peaceful, but this calmness is due to an avoidance of situations that trigger their emotions rather than true peace of mind. They are engaged in a pre-emptive strike; their avoidant behavior itself is their emotional reactivity.

The avoidant person needs to learn to identify avoidant behaviors and to stop them. Awareness of these behaviors is difficult because the rationalizations behind them are so complete. The individual engages in excuse making, judgments and other defense mechanisms not only to justify avoidance, but to disguise it. A person may even get so far away from his emotions that he no longer feels them, even in situations that would typically trigger intense emotions. Some people talk about serious abuse in their childhood as if they were reporting on someone else's childhood. Sometimes a person may express incongruous behaviors, such as laughing when they describe how they were physically abused as children. This dissociation from one's feelings occurs in many people who have had overwhelming trauma.

Facing Areas of Discomfort Gradually

To reclaim the emotional territory that he has lost, the avoidant person must develop a risk-taking philosophy for his emotional life. Many people fit the avoidant personality style—they are driven by fear and have high anxiety. For example, Mary had a difficult time standing up for herself. She had a series of bad relationships with men who did not treat her well. When someone asked her out for a date, she was unable to say "no" even though intuitively she knew the person was not good for her. So she always accepted, fearing she would hurt someone's feelings or cause conflict if she didn't. After getting involved with someone, she would make excuses to avoid having to break up with him, telling herself that the man had potential, that he would change, that she couldn't find anyone better. All these excuses occurred so that she did not have to experience conflict or loneliness.

For decades, behavioral therapists have used a technique called systematic desensitization, or gradual exposure, to help people cope with anxiety and phobias. This set of techniques has proven to be highly effective. Those with anxiety are taught to gradually expose themselves to the situations that cause them fear. Instead of being overwhelmed by facing their fears all at once, they take on their fears a little bit at a time. By facing fears slowly, they don't become overwhelmed.

Discomfort and distress

An avoidant person lives within a circle of comfort. Everything outside this circle is uncomfortable, and is avoided. Some of the situations outside of the circle may indeed be overwhelming and beyond a person's present capabilities to handle. For instance, an agoraphobic person may be tired of being limited by her problem, so she decides to go shopping at the mall despite her agoraphobia. She takes this risk, but then has a panic attack and runs back to her circle of comfort — her home — and vows never to do that again. Taking risks that are overwhelming can easily backfire. However, taking small risks works wonders. In the picture below, there is a circle of low risk drawn around the circle of comfort. This outer circle allows growth, but it is not so far outside of the comfort zone to be overwhelming.

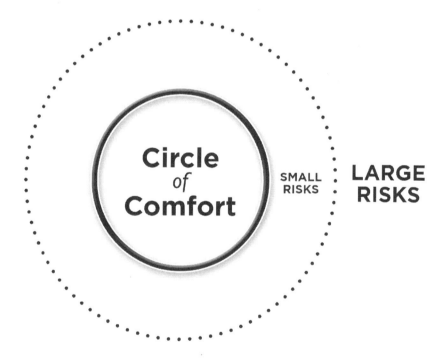

By continuously taking small risks outside the circle of comfort, the avoidant person can slowly face the fear and expand the circle of comfort. After a period of time, the circle of comfort may expand to the outer edge of what was the circle of small risks. They then must identify a new circle of small risks to expand their lives and their capabilities even further.

Each time the avoidant person takes a risk, they are brought face-to-face with an emotion they have been avoiding. This creates an opportunity to uncover emotions that were buried. Taking risks creates opportunities to bring up emotions that are difficult to contact any other way. By adopting this strategic risk-taking philosophy, an avoidant person may transform his life and expand its bounds appreciably. Consistent risk-taking can lead to facing psychological fears that have no basis in reality. If these feelings are embraced, then deep emotional healing can take place and can therapeutically transform the person over time.

For instance, Jerry had a difficult time admitting mistakes at work, defending himself even when he was wrong. He decided to confront this issue by taking small risks. He began by admitting mistakes to Al, his friend at work, whom he trusted. He found this uncomfortable at first because he felt shame about not being perfect. But he realized that although the emotion was uncomfortable, it was not overwhelming. This started Jerry on a journey of feeling more comfortable while admitting his mistakes, and led to many positive consequences in his life.

Everyone uses the strategy of avoidance at times to deal with uncomfortable emotions. It is not solely the province of the avoidant personality type. Facing areas of our lives that we avoid by taking consistent small risks is a tool we can all use. Those who are conflict-oriented may be avoiding feelings of vulnerability. A risk for them would be to check their anger, and allow their hidden, more vulnerable feelings to arise, thereby expanding their emotional range. Caretakers may need to face their fears of abandonment and the fear that arises when they trust that their loved ones can care for themselves. All of us need to take emotional risks; we can do this if we identify our avoidant behaviors and stop avoiding. This will bring us face to face with our unfelt emotions.

Using Fear as a Guide

Fear may be used as a guide to the areas of our lives in which we need to take risks. There are two types of fears. One is physical. We are afraid of heights for good reason—we could fall and hurt ourselves. The other type of fear is psychological: We may be afraid to speak in front of a group, but we are not in physical danger. Attuning ourselves to our psychological fears, and noticing them as they arise, gives us a handy navigation tool that tells us where we need to take risks in our lives. Learning to deal with our emotions also means that we are no longer held hostage by fear and avoidance.

Over the course of our lives we lose areas of feeling because of our defenses and avoidances. As children, we were open and in contact with our feelings and the world around us, but because of painful experiences we shut down to avoid further pain. As we grow older, we lose touch with our feeling nature, and whole areas of our lives suffer. Most notably, we lose intimacy in our families and in our romantic relationships. If we embrace our feelings, we may recover this lost territory of feeling. This will affect our happiness in many unsuspected ways. We may respond more to the world around us, because we can feel it more profoundly. Not only do our relationships improve, but so does our sense of being in the world. We are more connected to our bodies, our loved ones, other people and the culture around us. This heightened awareness of our emotions and feelings has political implications and is one of the main paths for humanity to heal as a group. When we are more emotionally sensitive, we are less likely to act out our aggression on other people. We also gain the capacity for more compassion. If others in our world are being hurt, we can be more responsive to them. We become more responsive to all human relationships.

Mindfulness

A technique that is helpful in embracing emotions is mindfulness. This is a Buddhist practice that is used to enhance and develop awareness. A Buddhist monk may practice mindfulness while he is cooking dinner or washing dishes. It is a helpful technique for spiritual development that is well-suited to busy Western lifestyles. It is also a great practice for anyone who would like to be able to handle their feelings more effectively. Our point of attention is usually focused on the content of our thinking. We think all day long and are absorbed in this thinking. Most of the time, we are not even aware we are thinking. The problem is that the content of our thinking is the source of our problems, at least psychologically. When we examine our thinking, we find that we utilize different kinds of thinking during the day. There is the practical, problem-solving kind that helps plan our day, such as "I need to stop at the bakery to pick up some bread on the way home," and there is the creative kind that supports these practical ideas and makes them happen. Neither of these is involved in psychological problems.

Ego-centered thoughts are what create suffering for us. Worry, for instance, is ego-centered thinking that has an adverse effect on our bodies because it creates stress. Here are some examples of this type of thinking, "I wonder how I'm doing compared to Joe." "I really need to have more money to be happy." "I can't stand that guy at the gas station." We may unfortunately engage in this type of thinking all day long. Ego-centered thinking focuses on protecting the concept of self or attacking others in order to feel better. If we think we are perfect and someone criticizes us, then we become indignant. We may also judge others to make ourselves feel better, or may even attack ourselves and put ourselves down. This type of thinking causes pain, creates stress in the body, and reinforces a separation between us and the world.

Mindfulness is a method to diminish this thinking and to focus our attention on something besides the stream of incessant thoughts that go through our minds all day long, causing us stress. The technique teaches us to attend to other areas of our experience. One of these areas is our sensations. While you are reading this, many sensations are occurring in your body. If you are sitting, you may feel the chair against your back and the lower part of your body. The air in the room may be felt on your face and the exposed parts of your body, and you may feel your feet on the floor. All these sensations are occurring constantly, but because they are so constant we do not pay attention to them. They become part of our background experience. We can bring them to our awareness at any time, however. When we do this we take some or all of our attention away from our thinking — the source of our psychological woes — to a place inside of us that is neutral psychologically. Focusing on our sensations allows us to experience peace and calm.

Another helpful area to become mindful of is our breath. Our breath is a constant background sensation that we rarely pay attention to. While breathing, many sensations are occurring — the rising and falling of our chests, the cool air hitting our nostrils. Breathing can be useful to focus on because it occurs in the part of the body where we feel the most intense emotions—between our nostrils and our stomachs. We describe emotions with such phrases as a "sinking in my stomach," "a tightness in my chest," "a heaviness in my heart," etc. In an effort to control our emotions, we may constrict these areas of our body, and consequently restrict our breathing. Deep breathing helps us to relax. By becoming more aware of our breath, we can make these automatic defenses more conscious. Then we have choice.

Mindfulness of sensations can be practiced anytime and anywhere — whenever your mind is not engaged in activities that need all of your attention. A good time to practice mindfulness is when there is nothing else to do and you would like to do something productive. For instance, waiting in line at a grocery store is a good place to practice, or while being stuck at a stoplight while driving. While walking or jogging or during any exercise, we can attend to the sensations in our bodies as we move.

By mindfulness of sensations, we become more aware of our bodies. This awareness prepares us to be more in touch with our feelings when they occur, since feelings are made up of sensations occurring in our bodies. If we practice mindfulness at times of the day when we are calm, then we are more prepared when a strong emotion does occur. Due to the deep relaxation that accompanies mindfulness practice, our baseline physiological state becomes less tense and more relaxed. We create the habit of bringing awareness to our bodies. This greatly improves our capacity to embrace our emotions and to contain them. We also experience a greater sense of being centered, and of not losing control of our behavior. We learn to soothe our own feelings by embracing them with our mindfulness.

Awareness When We Are Emotionally Aroused

By becoming more aware of our bodies we may learn to recognize when we are getting angry, fearful or distressed. Many people have a difficult time identifying these feelings until it's too late and the emotions have already become extreme. Intense emotions are much more difficult to handle. By having a greater sense of our bodies, we are more aware of the field in which these emotions express themselves. This gives us an edge. We experience these feelings arising in our bodies before they get unwieldy. When we become aware of an emotion as it is arising, we are more capable of soothing ourselves, and of acting more appropriately. It creates a space in which we can see how we are thinking about the situation and to see if our thinking is accurate.

Jeff and Sue have many petty arguments about how they plan to redecorate their house. They each have strong ideas and squabble over their differences. Jeff finds these arguments painful and a waste of time. He decides to practice mindfulness to focus more attention on his body, and to tune into his feelings. He begins to be more aware of when he is getting angry.

When he does this, he notices changes in his level of arousal, and this helps him to change his behavior when he and Sue disagree with each other. His presence of mind helps him change his communication and calm the situation rather than contribute to emotional reactivity. Sue was not able to do this as easily as Jeff. She had a more difficult time, but she did appreciate that Jeff was learning to do this, and she found herself less reactive because Jeff was less reactive.

Awareness and Choice

By practicing mindfulness, we not only help transform our uncomfortable feelings, we also increase our capacity to act more constructively. The behavior that is expressed during emotional reactivity is pre-programmed from the past, and is subconscious and automatic. But this automatic expression may be modified if people are aware of their body.

Awareness gives them a choice—they can choose a behavior based on the current situation, rather than one that was learned as a child.

If a friend walks into your room speaking in a loud voice with his fists clenched, you assume he is angry or very excited. He may be so angry or excited that he is not aware he appears threatening. If you ask him, "Are you angry?" he may say "yes" or "no" depending on his level of awareness of his emotions. If you ask him why his fists are clenched, he may stop to realize that they are clenched. At this point, he has a choice to keep his fists clenched or not. Before you pointed them out, he was unconscious of his fists. We have more choice once we bring a behavior into our field of awareness. When our attention is limited, partial, and focused on something else, we have less awareness and therefore fewer choices. Strong emotions can limit our awareness to a narrow field. Mindfulness and awareness of our bodies will help keep the field of awareness open or even expand it.

People Vary in Their Capacity to Experience Their Feelings

For some people feelings are readily accessible. Others, however, have a more difficult time getting in touch with their feelings, possibly due to different family backgrounds and cultural experiences. Some people grow up in families where both parents are mature in dealing with emotions. They learn to be in touch with their feelings from their parents. Other people grow up in families in which the parents are out of touch with their feelings. These parents are unable to teach their children this awareness. Others have traumatic things happen in their lives. This pain leads them to shut down their feelings. This is unfortunate. People who bury their feelings need to re-contact them to handle their emotions successfully. It is difficult to have successful relationships without this skill.

The ability to feel our emotions is a skill that needs to be relearned. We have it as a child. However, it is important to understand that people may differ hugely in their emotional expression. Some people are very effusive with their emotions and others are less expressive. Some of this is due to inborn predisposition. However a person expresses them, it is important that they can feel their emotions fully.

The Subtle World of Emotional Communication

As stated before there are two levels of communication — the rational verbal level and the emotional level. Even though people have little awareness of emotional communication, they end up responding to it much more than they think. Greater awareness of emotions helps you identify the emotions of people around you, and the emotional influence others have on you. When emotions become strong enough, rational thinking recedes into the background of awareness, and our emotions move into the foreground of consciousness.

We are influenced emotionally all the time by the environment and are mostly oblivious to this influence. Experts in public relations and propaganda understand the power of the emotional level of communication and our susceptibility through our emotions. Advertising influences our desires; political messages influence our fear and anger reactions. The most potent emotional communications come from those that are closest to us, however. They know us the best and we have history with them. The challenge is to catch these emotional communications before they affect us and make us act in ways that are counterproductive. Because people we are closest to know us so well, they also have greater ability to manipulate our emotions.

It is helpful to become aware of these influences before we get emotionally reactive. This can be difficult for a number of reasons. A person's words and "rational" communication may be at odds with what they are communicating to us emotionally. We get lost in the words and don't sense what is happening on the feeling level. It may be hard to identify when people are manipulating us emotionally, because they have no conscious desire to manipulate us; they are caught in their own emotional reactivity and have no idea what affect they are having on us. We may also be so wrapped up in our reasons for what we are saying or doing that we are not paying attention to the emotional level of communication.

Here are some questions we can ask ourselves to help discover this more subtle, emotional level of communication. You may want to consider a relationship that confuses you emotionally while you ask yourself these questions:

- What emotional pattern are we enacting together right now?
- Has this pattern occurred before? Is it habitual and difficult for us to extricate ourselves from?

- Am I feeling pressure emotionally from this other person to feel a particular way or to do something?

- What is the major emotion that I am feeling with this person? Is it anger, fear, guilt, shame, anxiety, hurt or another emotion? How does feeling this emotion make me want to act? How would this action contribute to the habitual pattern I have with this other person?

- How are we affecting each other with the emotions that we are expressing? Are these emotions affecting me in a manner that diverts me from what I really want?

- Can I remain aware of my feeling without acting or saying something according to the old script?

Attending to this hidden emotional level of communication can be a challenging task. However, becoming aware of this is one of the skills necessary to be able to master emotional reactivity and to insure we are not emotionally manipulated by others. Being mindful of our body not only helps us with emotional reactivity but with many other problems, also. Studies of mindfulness have shown it to help alleviate problems such as anxiety, depression, and personality disorders, as well as providing a general sense of well-being.

Chapter Key Points

- Many people have developed the habit of avoiding their emotions, but they need to embrace their emotions to allow them to heal

- There are six steps we can take to embrace our emotions.

- Practicing mindfulness is a useful technique that helps us stay with our emotions.

- If our emotions are scary to us, we can learn to embrace them a little at a time.

- Awareness of the subtle emotional level of communication is necessary to navigate our relationships with others.

EXERCISES

1. Bring your awareness to the sensations in different parts of your body. Get to know your feelings and sensations you feel by practicing this mindfulness.

2. Notice your breath. Feel your chest and diaphragm rise and fall with each breath. Feel the air go into your lungs. Notice the air hit your nostrils and how it feels as it goes in and out of your lungs.

Practice these exercises at various times during the day. Train yourself to check in with your body to see how it is feeling.

Try to be aware of the next time you get emotionally reactive by focusing on the arousal of feelings in your body. Particularly, notice the rising of negative feelings like anger, fear, shame, guilt, hurt, grief and distress. Stay with these feelings as they arise and bring your full awareness to them. Actively explore them with your awareness rather than running from them. See how this awareness affects your capacity to handle these situations.

CHAPTER 6

Step 5: Changing
Our Thinking

*"Your emotions are the slave of your thoughts,
and you are the slave to your emotions."*
ELIZABETH GILBERT, *Eat, Pray, Love:
One Woman's Search for Everything
Across Italy, India, and Indonesia*

E motions appear to occur in response to situations. But this is not
quite true. We actually do not respond emotionally to situations
themselves, instead, we become emotional over our thoughts about a
situation. When our view of a situation changes, our emotions change,
too. The following couple's experience illustrates this principle: Jean
was angry at her husband, Lucien, because of his unwillingness to spend
time with her family. Whenever activities were planned that included
her mother, father, brothers and sisters, Lucien either refused to go or he
made up excuses for why he could not attend. This was frustrating to Jean

because she felt that Lucien was unreasonable and was putting her in a position in which she had to choose between him and her family.

In couple's counseling, Lucien admitted that he felt embarrassed around Jean's family because they were all intelligent and well-educated. Lucien had dropped out of high school and later earned a G.E.D. Although, he did get a good job as a plumber, he was ashamed of his lack of education. In therapy he admitted to Jean that his discomfort was caused by his belief that he was not smart or sophisticated enough for her family. He said he liked them and that they never treated him badly, but he didn't like being around them because of his discomfort. Jean had never known that Lucien felt so much embarrassment about his educational level. He had always expressed himself so confidently around her. When she understood why Lucien had a problem being around her family, her anger evaporated. It changed to compassion for Lucien. Jean's feelings changed completely even though not much changed about the situation itself. Lucien still did not feel comfortable around her family, but Jean's view of the situation changed. She saw Lucien as struggling with his feelings rather than being stubborn or not liking her family. This change in view was all that was needed for Jean's anger to change to compassion.

The fourth major component of an emotion, besides behavior, feeling and sensation, is cognition or thinking. We have to have some thought about a subject before we can react emotionally to it. Usually our thinking is automatic, happens quickly, and is difficult to notice. When we react with fear because someone pulls out in front of us while we are driving, the thinking has already been established.

We know that the car pulling out in front of us presents a threat. Without this knowledge there would be no fear. An infant has no knowledge of cars or the damage they can do. A baby strapped into an car seat in the same situation would show no fear. Their ability to distinguish what is dangerous has not yet been learned. We cannot get upset about something without the involvement of this cognitive, thinking component.

What distinguishes emotional reactivity from normal emotions is that the perceptions of situations are distorted. Ideas about situations do not fit the reality of them. Because this distorted thinking is such an integral part of emotional reactivity, it is imperative that thinking is changed in an effort to reduce or eliminate ER. Little change can take place unless the distorted views are changed. There are two basic areas in which thinking gets distorted and causes emotional reactivity. One is when an emotional reaction is not based on facts. The second is when a situation is taken much more personally than it needs to be.

Is What You're Thinking True?

We may become emotionally reactive if we do not have our facts straight. We can get very upset over something that is pure fantasy. If someone tells Jack that his best friend "has an eye on his wife," he may become very upset and jealous, even though this information may be totally untrue. Perhaps his acquaintance was mistaken in his facts. It is very important for Jack to check out such a serious accusation before acting on it. If he finds out that the accusation is untrue, then his jealousy and fear of losing his wife to his best friend may disappear completely and immediately. The strong emotional reaction that he had when he thought it was true was based entirely on mistaken thinking.

It is very important to always check the information that our emotions are based upon. Emotionality depends much more on how we view a situation than on what is actually happening. This can be demonstrated by dreams. We can become very emotional in response to dreams, even though they are only a set of images going through our minds. I can wake up from a dream and feel very fearful because a lion was ready to kill me. I may wake up with my legs kicking, my heart pounding, and my body sweating — all based on the images going through my mind. This reaction to images in our mind can happen in waking life also. We need to make sure that our thinking reflects reality.

If we only had to distinguish what was real by checking out facts, we would have an easier time with our emotional reactivity. Unfortunately, experiences and beliefs from the past play a major part in distorting our thinking. Emotional learning is a way that the past can influence our present. When it is based on something real, it works very well in protecting us. I may have had experiences in the past with deceitful people manipulating me. The emotional learning that took place in that situation will make me cautious in dealing with similar people in the future. I will experience an immediate emotional note of caution that will inform me that I need to proceed cautiously around people with similar characteristics. This past emotional learning informs my present circumstance.

Negative Beliefs From the Past

When we are emotionally reactive, past learning leads to beliefs that are distorted in some manner. This distortion gets projected on the present event and causes emotional reactivity. We fail to see the present circumstances for what they are due to our past wounds. These past wounds created a change in our deep beliefs about ourselves and the world. These are called core beliefs.

Distortions in core beliefs center around four major areas: ourselves, our capabilities, others, or the world. Negative beliefs about ourselves make us think that we are bad, worthless, undeserving, or defective in some way. Negative beliefs about our capabilities cause thoughts of incompetence and lack of confidence in our ability to do things. Negative beliefs about others make us feel that we cannot trust others and we expect that we will be hurt or abused by them in some way. Negative beliefs about the world focus on the world as being unsafe, unfair, unpredictable, and painful.

When one of these sets of beliefs is triggered it becomes difficult for us to examine whether something is true or not, because we believe our core belief so completely. Core beliefs remain largely unquestioned. Those who have been injured often in their lives can develop very negative beliefs from these experiences. If the injury came through abuse, then all four areas may be affected. A child who has been physically, sexually or emotionally abused may pick up negative messages about themselves that tell them they are worthless, they are incompetent, they should never trust anyone, and that the world is a horrible place to be. With long-term abuse in one's background it may take many months of work to ferret out these negative beliefs, question their validity, and replace them with positive beliefs. Individuals who have been subjected to this kind of abuse can often best overcome their negative core beliefs with the aid of a trained psychotherapist.

We All Have Negative Beliefs

Even those of us who have come through our childhoods relatively unscathed develop negative beliefs that can limit our lives. We may not become all we can be or enjoy the depth of happiness possible for us. It may be difficult to notice negative beliefs because they remain beneath our consciousness. But if we become aware of these negative beliefs, we can access our negative programming and change. This access point occurs when we are emotionally reactive. At these moments, our negative beliefs come to the surface and take over for a short while. These painful moments offer an opportunity to work on ourselves and change these underlying beliefs that are difficult to access. Otherwise, we could erroneously assume that we have no problem in this area.

Most people have access to their negative beliefs during periods of high negative emotion, such as when suffering a great loss or experiencing a failure. During the vulnerable time after receiving news of a failure, old ideas and beliefs about our inadequacies, worthlessness, and distrust of others may arise. For a short time even the healthiest person may hate the world or their lives in reaction to the pain they are going through. Though these periods may be short-lived in individuals with mostly positive beliefs, they do demonstrate that everybody has some work to do in this area. Those who examine their episodes of emotional reactivity, ferret out the negative beliefs involved, and change them create a great opportunity for healing and growth for themselves.

Ed and Lisa both have negative beliefs from their pasts that trigger their emotional reactivity. Ed is very jealous. He accuses Lisa of flirting with others and having her eye on other men. Ed sometimes believes that Lisa is going to leave him. This belief comes from the emotional abuse that Ed received as a child. He was told in a number of ways that he was not a good, deserving person. This makes him feel that he does not deserve Lisa. Besides emotional abuse, one of Ed's experiences in childhood was that his mother cheated on his dad. This led him to believe that women are not to be trusted in marriage. Sometimes, he is fine and does not think these jealous thoughts. Other times, he is overwhelmed by his jealousy of Lisa and becomes very angry and accusatory.

Lisa reacts to Ed's accusations by getting furious at him and criticizing him for being so jealous. Their arguments become superheated. Ed's anger reminds her of her father's rages that, though they were rare, were terrifying to her in her childhood. This makes it intimidating for Lisa to deal with Ed when he becomes so angry.

Because Lisa was highly motivated and had less negative conditioning in her background, she was able to make the first moves in working on her own emotional reactivity. She realized that Ed's jealousy was Ed's problem. She was not doing anything wrong, and she did not need to defend herself so strongly when he became jealous. She also realized that Ed was not her father. This change in thinking helped her to see the problem more clearly. Although she still felt some anger when Ed accused her of cheating, she was able to act and communicate much more effectively with Ed.

Lisa also realized that Ed's background led him to believe these things about her. Through examining her own emotional reactivity, she learned that Ed was thinking in a distorted manner due to his past. This enabled her to change her way of dealing with him. Instead of criticizing him when he became jealous, she reassured him instead. She learned to ask him in a loving manner if he would work on his jealousy. When Ed began to get a different reaction from Lisa—she no longer seemed so defensive—he also became less upset when they talked about the subject. Because his attention no longer needed to be focused on defending his position, Ed could begin looking at himself. Slowly, he began to take more responsibility for his jealousy. As he did this, his jealous outbursts became less and less common, and their relationship became more loving.

Lisa no longer worried that she would have to leave Ed because of his anger and jealousy. By reducing her own emotional reactivity, she opened a path for Ed to reduce his own. This is not always the case, but it is amazing how often this happens. More times than not, one person working on their ER leads to at least some healing in the whole relationship. Ed could have refused to take responsibility for his jealousy and his distorted thinking. Even so, Lisa still would have gained from the situation. She would have changed her own emotional reactivity. If she had ended up divorcing Ed, the capacity to handle her ER would have helped in her future relationships.

Exaggeration

Sometimes, the distortion in our thinking about a situation is not false, but our thinking is exaggerated and we may draw faulty conclusions. For instance, it may be true that our spouse has a problem being neat, but we may exaggerate this in our minds. We may think that he or she is always sloppy and not notice anytime that our spouse is neat. We turn something that is annoying into something that is overwhelming. This exaggeration triggers emotional reactivity. If we kept perspective on the issue we could reduce our emotional reactivity considerably. It sometimes happens that one person wants a divorce because they have exaggerated the behavior of the spouse so greatly that they cannot live with them anymore, but once this person reduces their exaggeration and sees their spouse more clearly, they may work more effectively on the issue.

Faulty Conclusions

Sometimes problems arise from drawing faulty conclusions about a problem. Nancy believed that because Dave did not like to dress up and go out with her, that he did not love her. Dave's dislike of formal events was factual, but had little to do with his love for her.

But Nancy's conclusion that this meant Dave did not love her led to such intense emotional reactivity that it jeopardized the relationship. Once Nancy questioned this faulty conclusion, she reduced her emotional reactivity, and was able to work on this difference more constructively with Dave. As the emotional reactivity diminished, the couple could discuss the situation with a more cooperative attitude and find mutually satisfying solutions.

Taking It Personally?

Besides asking ourselves if what we are thinking is true, we need to look at how personally we react to an issue. We may take things personally more often than is necessary. Taking things personally contributes directly to the intensity of any emotion. If we work at a factory and hear of another factory closing in the next town, we probably will not respond with much fear. The fear becomes much greater if the factory that is closing is the one where we are working. Obviously, the closer a negative event is to us, the more we get upset. The prospect of being laid off is a personal challenge and can be upsetting, but if a faulty conclusion is made, like, "I'll never get a good job like this again," then the event is even more upsetting. The conclusion that we have drawn is not only a faulty one, but is also a highly personal one. It exaggerates the negative effect that the factory closing will have on us.

Learning to take things less personally helps reduce emotional reactivity. Sophie had a critical partner, Omar, who could always find something to complain about. This was painful for Sophie because her parents had also been critical of her, and Omar's criticisms triggered her past wounds. When Omar was critical, Sophie would get defensive by either shutting down or striking back at Omar with her own criticisms. She reacted to Omar's remarks in a number of ways that made it more difficult for her. She made it more personal than it needed to be. She felt inferior when she made mistakes and thought that because Omar criticized her that she was unlovable. She had strong beliefs in her own incompetence. Omar's attitude reinforced these personal areas of negative belief.

Sophie began working on her emotional reactivity. The first thing she did was to look at how she personalized criticism to an exaggerated extent. She then began to realize that Omar's criticism was not because there was something wrong with her, but that Omar had a problem with being too critical. This helped her take some of the pressure off of herself. She also began to examine the wound she had received from her critical parents. She realized that she was not at fault for developing that wound, but it was her responsibility to change it. She started to question her belief in her own incompetence and began to pat herself on the back for some of her accomplishments. She realized that she had been too hard on herself. When she recognized that Omar had a problem with being too critical, she realized that this was not because of his lack of love for her, but because he was deeply wounded himself. All of these changes in Sophie's outlook helped her take Omar's criticism less personally and reduced her emotional reactivity.

Our View Affects Everything

How we view our lives affects everything that we do—emotionally and physically. It affects our behavior, our success in life, and even our perception. We perceive as important only those things in the world that reinforce our pre-conditioned view of it. If you view yourself as unlovable and walk into a room where half the people smile at you and half of them frown, the tendency will be to only notice the people who are frowning. This perception matches your view that you are unlovable. If you believe that you are lovable and walk into the same room, you may only notice the people who are smiling at you. The smilers are more visible because their smiles go along with who you think you are. Our worldview is intimately connected with how we live our lives.

Our view is composed of all the beliefs we have about ourselves, our abilities, others, and the world. It is important to understand what our beliefs are about our lives, so that we can change them if they are negative. Because many beliefs are subconscious, we need to bring them to the surface to change them. Times of emotional reactivity are a wonderful opportunity to do this work. Our negative beliefs come to the surface without us having to try to dig for them.

Views That Interfere with Changing Our Behavior

We cannot make changes in ourselves or heal emotionally without stopping negative acting out. Certain core beliefs get in the way and hinder out ability to do this. One belief system that is problematic is the need to be always tough or macho. This belief limits one's choices in life and makes it difficult to access more vulnerable emotions. The macho person feels compelled to be strongly assertive in any situation. This leads to rigid behavior—one can only act tough. Opportunities to develop and express more vulnerable emotions are ignored. By always trying to be powerful, the person actually loses power because true power is based on the ability to act in any manner that is appropriate to a situation. If one can only act in a strong manner, that power actually is diminished. This can lead to many difficulties with emotional reactivity and even violence.

Another belief that prohibits a change in emotionally reactive behaviors is the idea that we must always put on a front of some kind to hide certain emotions. Many people believe they will lose the support of others if they show their feelings. This is not necessarily true, and needs to be questioned. Or they may feel that if they drop their guard and reveal more vulnerable emotions, their partner will take advantage of their display of weakness and use it against them. Usually the opposite of this actually takes place. By allowing ourselves to communicate more vulnerable feelings, our partners will feel safer and encouraged to discuss their feelings. It moves both partners away from the tendency to only express anger toward each other.

Views That Interfere with Embracing Our Feelings

It can be difficult to embrace the feeling component of an emotion because of various distorted beliefs. One such belief is that if we allow ourselves to feel an emotion, it will be so overwhelming that we will not be able to handle it. We may fear that we would go crazy or "lose it." Actually, no feeling can "make" us go crazy. Usually the difficulties that people have in embracing their emotions come more from negative beliefs about the emotion than from the intense feelings in their bodies. We can have very negative beliefs about experiencing our feelings. We believe that we will be unable to stand the emotion, that it will overwhelm us, or that we will lose control. Beliefs that increase our fear of our emotional states need to be challenged. If our experience has been that we do get overwhelmed by our emotions and act in ways we regret, then it is important for us to believe that we can gain the skills necessary to handle our emotions better. When we have negative beliefs about our emotions, we will exacerbate our tendency to avoid emotion through acting out and other self-destructive behaviors.

Notice Your Self-Talk When You Get Emotionally Reactive

Self-talk or automatic thoughts occur every time we are emotionally reactive. If we can listen carefully to this self-talk it will tell us how we view a particular situation, and we will learn how this self-talk contributes to our reactions. During an upsetting argument our self-talk tends to be inflammatory. We say things to ourselves like, "How dare they..." "Who do they think they are?" "I can't stand it." "I'll show them." "Nobody talks to me that way." All these self comments are like dry logs thrown onto the fire of our anger and outrage. It can be argued that these inflammatory statements are more responsible for our anger than the situation itself. They get us so upset that it is impossible to think or act appropriately.

Instead, we need to get into the habit of using self-talk that calms us down, such things as: "I'm going to remain calm." "I'm not going to let her get to me." "I don't have to let this upset me." "I'm not going to give him the power to manipulate my emotions." Statements like these make it easier to remain calm.

Other self-comments help us take things less personally. For instance, saying, "I don't have to take this personally," can be helpful. Or "This is his problem, not mine. I don't have to make it mine." "I am not the one that is calling names here." "I don't have to take on that name." When another person acts poorly we refuse to take it as meaning that there is something wrong with us.

Developing a Coping Statement for Difficult Situations

When we know we are going to be in a difficult situation, we can develop a coping statement prior in advance—a statement that jars our thinking back to clarity about the situation. For example, Joe, like many people, was sensitive to criticism. When his wife, Gail, asked him to change his behavior in any way, he typically became angry and defensive. This was frustrating for Gail because she could not communicate to Joe things that she thought were important to change. When not in Gail's presence, Joe could think more clearly about this situation and see that his defensiveness was hurting their relationship.

In his efforts to overcome his emotional reactivity, Joe developed a more realistic series of thoughts—thoughts to help him not take the situation so personally. His more appropriate thinking went something like this:

"Gail has the right to communicate to me, even to bring things up about my behavior that she doesn't like. I have the right to agree or disagree with her. It's just conversation. I don't have to take it personally. I can think it over and decide what I am going to do with the information she gives me. If my behavior is wrong, then the only right thing to do is to change it."

This mode of thinking helped Joe develop a set of coping statements to deal with Gail's feedback about his behavior, and it enabled him to listen to her without getting defensive. He was able to calm himself down and be much less emotionally reactive to Gail. Gail toned down her criticisms and became less judgmental.

Developing coping statements before entering into emotionally reactive situations works well. Once in the situation, we may be too upset to think clearly. It is better to explore our thoughts when we are calm, to decide how we view the situation that makes us so upset, and to develop a coping statement that is tailored for the situation. Coping statements are designed to help us look at situations in a more realistic light; they usually are different from what we have told ourselves before. Good coping statements have these qualities: they are truer and more realistic, they go directly against the distortions in our thinking that caused the problem in the first place, and they help us take the situation less personally.

Some people write their coping statements down on a piece of paper or a 3x5 card and keep it in their pocket for whenever the situation comes up. This allows them time to straighten out their thinking and consequently reduce their emotional reactivity. Putting the statements in writing is handy because we can easily fail to remember our skills when we get emotionally reactive. Emotional reactivity triggers regression to an old way of thinking that does not work.

For some, changing one's thinking during emotional reactivity is a difficult thing to do. They may have longstanding habits of putting themselves down or judging others. Their core beliefs may be very negative and pervasive. These individuals might have a hard time regulating their emotions because they are convinced on some level that they are being taken advantage of as they have been in the past. For people with such profound negative beliefs, psychotherapy may be helpful in gaining control over their emotional reactivity.

What is Thought?

Since we think continually, it is important to understand the limitations of our thoughts. Thoughts about reality are never reality itself, thoughts can only describe reality in an accurate, yet limited, way. My description of being at the Grand Canyon will never be able to convey the magnificence of that sight. Even if I am a great poet and able to convey a sense of majesty in my poem, the poem will always fall short of the experience. Thought is limited in its nature, yet there are many people who believe their thoughts are true just because they think them. They may never question the truth of their negative beliefs.

The habit of accepting distorted thinking is deeply ingrained. It is important to realize that our thoughts at best represent a dim reflection of the reality of our experience. Imagine trying to tell someone what sugar tastes like if they have never tasted sugar before.

It's Just a Story

We are always telling ourselves stories about events in our lives. We explain and give meaning to our lives through stories. Some of the themes go on and on throughout our lives. But at some level, these stories are limited, and our actual experience is quite open when there is no story. For instance, when we are out in nature and in awe of our surroundings, for a little while we are not in our story. We are experiencing the nature around us without interference from our thoughts. At these times we experience nature as it truly is and enjoy the peace that it brings. When we begin thinking again, our attention is drawn away from the natural surroundings and our experience again closes down.

In many ways we are like a novelist. We are writing a story with the main character as ourselves. We have to be very careful how we tell this story. Is it going to be a tragedy or a comedy? Many times from the first page of a novel, we can tell how the hero or heroine is going to end up by the way that character is described in the first few pages. Sometimes novelists surprise us and their characters change and grow and the inevitable tragedy is averted. We have the power to change our own stories. But in order to change and improve our stories, we need to become aware of how we are telling that story to ourselves in the first place.

Mindfulness of Our Thoughts and Emotions

Our minds can do the silliest things. If we are told not to think about something, we will think about it. If we feel guilty about certain thoughts, sooner or later they will pop into our minds. It is critical to realize that we do not have complete control over our thoughts. The problem is not that we think too much. Thinking tends to happen pretty much all the time. The problem is that we believe our thoughts unconditionally and assume that they are reality, when at best they can only attempt to describe what is real. The attempt may turn out to be wrong, yet we cling to these thoughts stubbornly, unwilling to let them go or question them.

One way to create some space in our minds and to lessen our attachment to our thoughts is to use a technique that was designed for this purpose, called *mindfulness of thoughts*. With this method we identify our thoughts rather than identify *with* them. If we can label our thoughts, we can gain some distance from our thinking as if we are watching them from the outside. If we have angry thoughts toward someone, it is difficult for these thoughts not to take us over, particularly if the anger is really strong. But if we can label them by saying something like, "There is an angry thought," or "There is a hateful thought," they become less potent for us. They cannot disturb us so easily when we separate ourselves from them. They have less power to control our lives and less capacity to incite emotional reactivity in us.

Pain Versus Suffering

It is important to make a distinction between psychological pain and psychological suffering. We do not experience psychological suffering except through our thinking. Occasionally, we experience pure, psychological pain—when we are abused, when we have a great loss, or when others are hurtful to us. However, suffering is created by distorted thinking, when we fail to see and accept the world as it is.

It is common for people to understand intuitively that thinking is the source of their suffering. When we are not thinking, we are usually at peace. Some people try to dull their thinking through alcohol or drugs to gain temporary peace of mind. Numerous people with alcohol addiction report that the attractive thing about alcohol is that it shuts down their tortured thinking. Other people become deeply involved in activities, to distract them from thinking about themselves. Workaholism and other "busy-ness" addictions are examples of how people are compelled to keep their thoughts on some practical project outside of themselves as a means to avoid thinking about their problems.

It is not a problem to be busy, but it is a problem to ruminate in a torturous manner. There is no other cause of psychological suffering besides our thinking. Other things may cause us physical and psychological pain, but psychological suffering is an inside job. Our strong, negative feelings become exaggerated when we dwell on them. We may lose somebody and feel grief; our tears show that we loved that person. This is a pure emotional pain. We create a psychological overlay of suffering on this pain when we tell ourselves a negative story about this event. We feel the grief, but we also tell ourselves, "I'll never be happy without this person in my life." "I can't live without him." "Life is unfair." What we tell ourselves leads to greater suffering. We take the pain that is natural to the situation — grief — and add a dimension of unnecessary suffering on top of it.

Our suffering is due to imposing a conceptual overlay onto our personal experience. We do not accept reality as it is, but impose thoughts on it of how it should be. I should be different. Others should be different. Life should be different. This imposition of *should* on things can work in the outer world as far as objects are concerned. We can look at a painting on the wall and say that it should be straight and then straighten it. No problem. The problem occurs when we try to impose these *shoulds* on things that are not easy to change or are not going to change, such as ourselves, others, past events, or the world. Acceptance is paramount with these things. Even though we can change aspects of the world, or ourselves, we need to start these projects with acceptance of "what is". We have to begin with reality.

It is important that we develop the skill of questioning our thinking. Our minds can and will become out of balance if we do not. There is no telling what crazy thoughts will pop into our minds. If we believe everything that we think, we have lost control of one of the most important navigation instruments in life. Peace of mind only comes to those who have mastered their own thinking. There is no abiding peace of mind for those controlled by distorted thinking.

CHAPTER KEY POINTS

- Our emotions are determined by our interpretations of events. Make sure that you interpretations are true.

- We have negative beliefs from the past that interfere with seeing events in the present clearly.

- Taking things too personally leads to emotional reactivity.

- Negative beliefs about changing our behavior or embracing our emotions inhibit healthy functioning.

- Notice any distorted self-talk you may have in situations in which you get emotionally reactive. Develop a coping statement to help you in these situations.

EXERCISES

1. Think of a situation in which you become emotionally reactive. What are the thoughts that you have about this situation? Are these thoughts true? Are you sure? Are they exaggerated in any way?

2. Take the thoughts that you have identified in exercise one and change these to beliefs that are more workable in the situation. Correct them if they are distorted or exaggerated.

3. When you were emotionally reactive, did you find yourself taking what others said or did more personally than was necessary? Examine this and see what you can tell yourself that will help you take this less personally.

4. Develop a set of coping statements to help you be less emotionally reactive in this situation. Make sure you give yourself coping statements that help you take the situation less personally.

CHAPTER 7

STEP 6: Getting a "Black Belt": Containing Emotional Reactivity

"Practice is the best of all instructors."
PUBLIUS SYRUS

Mastering our emotional reactivity is a huge task that cannot be accomplished in one day. It takes practice. It's like the belt system in martial arts; it takes time. Usually we start with a white belt and then move through the colors to brown and then to black. The more we practice the techniques outlined in this book, the better we become at handling our ER. Once we start getting our emotional reactivity out of the way, communication and love can re-awaken in our relationships.

Review the steps outlined in this book and practice them. Insight is not sufficient for people to change. Many people know what they should change but do not do it. Ask anybody who has tried a diet plan and failed. We may know that our anger is out of

131

control, but that does not mean we have developed the ability to control our aggression. Practice is necessary.

True Insight Can Take Time and Practice

Mere intellectual insight can be very superficial. When we need to change a difficult problem in our lives, we usually have to hear about it, not once, but a hundred times. When I was smoking cigarettes in my youth, about every six months, I would say to myself that I should quit because it was expensive and bad for my health. After about three years, this insight and desire to quit became a daily understanding, and only then was I able to quit. Our insights require time to take hold and become deep enough to affect us.

Great religious traditions have an understanding of insight and how it leads to change. A monk may contemplate something for years. He will work with an idea over time, deepening his insight until his understanding grows enough to change his life. For instance, Catholic monks may contemplate the nature of the Trinity for a lifetime, Buddhists spend years contemplating the nature of impermanence, and Advaita Vedanta Hindus may spend years contemplating the question, "Who am I?" There is an understanding among religious people that to have a truly transformative insight, time and dedication are needed.

All of us have had to deal with our emotions from the time that we were children. Unless we have had very wise parents who handled their emotions well, we may have a problem with our emotions. It is unlikely our parents knew how to handle their emotions well, because our culture has been confused about emotions and how to deal with them. In the past, two different extreme views of managing emotions have been common. One is to express emotions even if it is hurtful to ourselves or others, and the other is to hold them in and control them regardless of the cost. Poor emotional habits come from caretakers who themselves have had poor emotional habits. Changing these old habits can lead to profound changes in our lives.

Prepare Yourself Ahead of Time

It is helpful to anticipate situations in which we become emotionally reactive. We know who it is that pushes our buttons. By identifying these people and situations, we can prepare ourselves and develop an intention to react differently.

When we are emotionally reactive a lessening of consciousness occurs, and we regress to an earlier mode of functioning. Old habits reassert themselves automatically. It is very helpful to prepare ourselves for this emotional arousal, so we can be alert rather than fall into unconsciousness. When emotionally reactive, we may feel attacked and want to strike out at whoever is triggering us. To break free of this old conditioning, we need to feel our bodies become emotionally reactive, and alert ourselves that we are in a situation that calls for a deepened awareness. Eventually we can develop a habit of associating high emotional arousal to alertness and readiness rather than unconscious behavior. Then, we can handle the situation in a different way.

It is unlikely that anyone can completely manage their emotional reactivity in one day. It truly is like getting a black belt in a martial art. We need to work with the techniques and practice them. For some people, the hardest thing for them to do will be to stop the old behavior; for others it will be the tendency to externalize, or to have distorted thinking, or to have difficulty being mindful of the feeling. Rereading those particular chapters can be helpful.

Putting It All Together

People who have their fight-or-flight reaction triggered may trigger us. We physiologically react to people when they are emotionally reactive. This is a protective mechanism that was designed for survival, because people who are highly reactive are more dangerous. We get aroused—ready to fight or to run away to protect ourselves.

Although this arousal is natural, it can be contained through mindfulness. By being aware of our sensations, behaviors, and thoughts we can stop this physiological disturbance from infecting the psychological realm. The physical upset we feel does not have to turn into psychological suffering. We can stop ourselves from getting swept up into psychological pain that makes us act and think in ways that make the situation worse.

134

Transforming Emotional Reactivity by Using Imagination

Besides practicing when the events that trigger our emotional reactivity are already upon us, you can practice before they occur in your imagination. What to do first is to imagine a situation in which you become emotionally reactive. You need to imagine it so well that some of the feeling we experience in that situation comes up for you. We can reprogram ourselves by imagining new responses and new behaviors. This creates an association between the arousal state and new ways of acting and thinking.

Sarah did some work in her imagination to try to be less emotionally reactive to her husband, John. She had a difficult time with his criticism and complaints. Because he put her down in the past, she had become sensitive to even minor complaints of his. She felt that she had become so sensitive that she had gone too far, and now was closed to anything that John said.

To work on this she imagined John criticizing her. Imagining this brought up feelings of hurt and anger. She reviewed her past behavior of attacking John when he did this, and saw that it was not working. She started with not externalizing. She wanted to take responsibility for her ER, and at the same time hold John accountable for his behavior if he was communicating in an abusive way. She needed to be clear about that boundary. She practiced holding John accountable for his faulty communication by confronting him appropriately about it in her imagination. She saw herself say the right words to

John. By going through the situation in her imagination, she became more confident and felt like she had a plan for the situation. Through this exercise she formed a new set of associations to her experience of John criticizing her. She began associating awareness, confidence, new behaviors, and new thinking with that situation. This exercise also helped her desensitize herself to the upsetting emotions that she felt. Being able to consciously face it in her mind reduced her fear of the situation.

The next time John criticized her she was alert. She could feel her level of arousal go up. Initially, she became defensive and struck out at John. However, she was able to reign in this old behavior. She apologized for what she said. She realized John was using a sarcastic tone and asked him not to do this with her. She explained that the sarcasm made it much more difficult for her to hear his feedback and was unnecessary. John got defensive about using that tone and accused her of being too sensitive. This activated Sarah again and she had to struggle to not get pulled into an all-out war. Sarah's responses to John's criticism were so different than usual that this affected John. Her poise gave him space to think about what he was doing rather than be defensive. He felt that Sarah was reaching out to him and this had a great impact on him. Because of the lower reactivity on Sarah's part, it was much easier for John to keep his emotional reactivity low and think more clearly about what he was doing. Sarah felt that she had been mostly successful in handling the situation in a new way and this gave her impetus to continue working on it in the future.

As Sarah practiced in her imagination and then with John, she began to de-condition her old reactions. She was helping to establish new learning pathways in her brain — ones that led to more consciousness in the situation, an ability to view the situation in a new light, and to behave very differently. At the same time, John was learning some of these skills from her, as she offered him an example of a new way to handle the situation. Interestingly, John began to change, and he never even heard the term emotional reactivity.

Working on Emotional Reactivity with Others

Work on emotional reactivity in a relationship moves much more quickly when both partners are doing it together. Mutual efforts reinforce each other. When couples are serious about changing their emotional reactivity and embrace this together, the swiftness of change in the relationship can be striking. It is important to understand that, whether your partner works on this or not, you can still benefit personally from working on emotional reactivity. Typically, you will find immediate benefits in your relationship when you have made these changes. This is not always the case, however. Sometimes we can be in relationship with people who are very emotionally reactive and are unwilling to take responsibility for this. These people create a poisoned emotional environment for those around them. They are so addicted to emotional reactivity that when presented with someone who is trying to change the interaction and make it more positive, they become more provocative. They try to draw the other person into the old habits of interaction. Luckily, most people are not so desperately addicted to their emotional reactivity. They do it simply because they know no alternative, and when they see a way out they take it.

If you are in a relationship with somebody who is highly reactive and does not seem like they want to change, a few things can be helpful.

See if your partner or family member will go to a therapist with you. Choose a therapist who is experienced at helping people work through their emotional reactivity.

1. Work on your own reactivity. One of the things that contributes to somebody being addicted to emotional reactivity is that they are successful in drawing others into that state. It will be very helpful for that person if you react as little as possible to them.

2. During states of calm in your relationship, see if you can get your family member to agree to work on this with you. This must be presented very carefully to that person.

3. Continue to practice. It is gratifying to develop the skills to defuse these painful situations. Transforming emotional reactivity can be a challenging thing to do for many people. If you find that you have read this book and tried these techniques, but you have trouble making progress, then you may want to work with a therapist on these ideas. You may find that you will have to do a period of personal work on yourself before you will be able to respond differently to difficult situations.

CHAPTER KEY POINTS

- Emotional reactivity is not overcome overnight. It takes practice.

- Imagine being in a situation in which you get emotionally reactive. Bring the feelings up and imagine handling the situation differently.

- See if you can encourage a person whom you get emotionally reactive with to work on this with you.

EXERCISE

Imagine a situation in which you become emotionally reactive. Imagine it so clearly that you can access some of the feelings that come up in that situation. Who are you with? Where are you? What are you saying to each other? Go through the whole situation, but imagine handling it much differently. Make sure you use all the steps outlined in this book to change the situation in your imagination. Imagine behaving more effectively; imagine holding the strong emotions and being very conscious of them; imagine talking to yourself in a different way about the situation — talk to yourself in a manner that is less negatively distorted.

CHAPTER 8

Step 7: Responding Compassionately

"Compassion is the basis of morality."
ARNOLD SCHOPENHAUER

Once we have gone through the previous six steps, we have set the stage for us to act with compassion in our relationships to others. Being lost in emotional reactivity is incompatible with acting compassionately. Compassion is a higher function. When we are emotionally reactive, our lizard brain takes over and short circuits the more evolved parts of the brain that can be compassionate. Compassion is one of the qualities that distinguishes humans from lower forms of animals.

When we act compassionately toward others, it is healing for them and helps them grow emotionally. By developing this trait in ourselves we not only benefit others close to us, but we benefit the world also. It becomes a better place. We can influence the environments we live in to be kinder and more respectful.

The benefits are not limited to others. Responding compassionately benefits us too, by improving our relationships to other people. My experience with people in my psychotherapy practice is that the people who are more giving to others are also happier. They are less self-concerned and suffer less. Studies in positive psychology support the idea that those who help others are happier. Seligman, in his book, *Authentic Happiness*, states that the highest type of satisfaction is when we are living a meaningful life, and one of the primary ways of living a meaningful life is through serving others in some way. Satisfaction surveys given to those involved in various jobs and professions consistently indicate that those serving others have the highest levels of satisfaction — as long as the job is not too stressful. Compassion is one of the skills necessary for success. It does not make a person weak, because traits such as having good boundaries, being honest and direct, not enabling others, and having the capacity to work toward goals are all compatible with compassion. One can remain tough-minded and realistic without being tough on others.

All Major Religions Encourage Compassion

Every great religion teaches us to aspire to demonstrate more compassion in our lives. In Christianity, the central teaching is to be compassionate. John (13:34) in his gospel reports on Christ's advice to us: "As I have loved you, so must you love one another." The great Christian philosopher Henry Nouwen, in his book with McNeil and Morrison, *Compassion: A Reflection on the Christian Life*, describes the importance of striving to be compassionate as the most important aspiration for a good Christian. They point out that it is not enough to know the teachings of Christ; one needs to live as Christ by treating others with the same compassion that he embodied.

In the East, Buddhism teaches that the practice of compassion is central to personal transformation. It is one of the fundamental practices leading to enlightenment. Buddhist teachers have devised many practices to train people to be compassionate. In one Tibetan Buddhist practice, you are encouraged to imagine yourself breathing in the sin and suffering of others so that you can relieve others of this burden and help purify them. In Hinduism, one of the major paths to enlightenment is karma yoga, which is the path of service. By dedicating our lives to serving others we overcome the selfish parts of our own nature and become more enlightened. Any parent or person who has dedicated themselves to serving other people knows how truly transformative this can be. You have to get out of your own way to be effective in helping others.

Major religions not only encourage us to be compassionate, their central figures are embodiments of compassion. Christ is the ultimate model of compassion, sacrificing himself for the benefit of others. In Islam, Allah is described as the most compassionate and merciful. In Buddhism, certain Buddhas are considered to be incarnations of compassion. In Hinduism, Hanuman is one of the Gods that embodies compassion and service. Hanuman, the monkey god, would do anything to serve Rama in his quest to set the world right.

In our culture it is easy to lose our way and believe that what we should strive for is more material goods, power, or money. One of the sources of true happiness and fulfillment comes from being compassionate and developing the wisdom that this necessitates. Studies have shown that once we have an income that affords us the basic necessities of life and pays our bills, having more does not increase our happiness much. When one practices compassion, there is no end to the benefits you receive.

One of the professional activities that I have been engaged in for over a decade is training beginning therapists. A therapist must learn to get his or her self-concerns out of the way so that he or she can truly listen to clients. I am amazed at the personal growth that my students go through in learning how to help others. They are challenged on a psychological level to change and open their hearts and minds by the activity of trying to help. Through my own experiences as a therapist and through the experiences of my students, it is apparent to me that learning to help others is one of the most potent means of self-transformation.

Developing an Intention to be Compassionate

Our behavior usually follows our intentions. Goals shape our lives and help us create pain or happiness for ourselves. Being intent on developing compassion can be a potent force in bending the course of our lives toward joy and contentment. If being compassionate is one of our highest values, then it will have the power to wake us up to opportunities to be kinder to others. It will help us penetrate the unconscious fog of emotional reactivity and guide us to interact with others more skillfully.

Skills Necessary for Compassionate Relationships

Paying Attention

Paying mindful attention to others is a key skill in responding compassionately. Mindful attention means we pay attention to others as they are, without the intervening screen of pre-conceived notions. Without a strong desire to see the person beyond our conceptions of them, we are inhibited from knowing and meeting the person as they are. This habit of filtering all our experience through pre-conceived notions makes it difficult to experience another person without this interference.

Attend to the other person without the mind wandering. Notice the difference between truly seeing the other person, or attending to your ideas about the person. If your mind wanders too much bring it back to seeing the person as they are in the moment.

While you are attending to somebody else, to be truly mindful you must also attend to the surroundings. The background environment is the second part of the field of your awareness of which you must be mindful. The third aspect of this field of awareness is awareness of self. By being aware of your emotions and sensations, you remain grounded in the situation and it is harder for your mind to wander away. Pay attention to the sensations in your body. Keep attention to yourself within the greater field of awareness as you listen to the other person. This helps you create a container for all possible reactions you can have to the other person as you listen to them. It allows you to stay conscious of your reactions so that you can choose to remain compassionate regardless of what the other person says—even when the other person says something that is potentially upsetting to you. Mindfulness of your body creates openness to others and at the same time saves you from being victim to the emotional manipulations of others.

We remain compassionate to others by remaining present in the situation. We are not reacting by getting upset or by avoiding. If we feel like avoiding or responding angrily, we are alert enough to see the initial impulse, contain it, and choose a response that is better for the situation. In this way our capacity to listen to others becomes as great as our capacity to be mindful and present. We expand the number of situations in which we can remain a compassionate presence.

The Skill of Listening

When we are mindful of others, we are capable of listening, which is a primary communication skill. Mindfulness frees us to listen, because we are not caught up in our own thinking and are able to pay attention. To truly listen to others, we can't be focused on what we are going to say in response to them. We are not thinking about something else while we nod politely as if we were truly paying attention. When we do think, the thinking does not take over our consciousness; it occurs without us losing awareness of the other person or of ourselves. Because we are aware of ourselves and are vigilant, we can think without getting lost in our thoughts.

By listening mindfully to another person, we pay attention to more than what the person says. We get cues to how the other person is feeling, what they want, and what they need. This depth of listening helps us become more empathic. We get more of a sense of what the other person is going through, and it becomes easier to imagine what it would be like to be in the other person's place. When we attend to another person so fully, an experience may arise of becoming one with them in some way. It is as if the distance of having separate bodies disappears because our souls are meeting.

To enhance our listening and to let the other person know that they are being heard, we use active listening. Verbal cues like, "Uh huh"and "I see," tell the other person we are following them and reassure them that they are being heard. Non-verbal cues like nodding are effective, also. Other active listening skills are:

Reflective listening in which you reflect back a part of what the person said to indicate to them that you are following them.

- Paraphrasing is a similar skill except that you put what they have said in your own words.
- Summarizing is the skill of taking a number of ideas and presenting a summary of these ideas back to the speaker. Sometimes this can be presented in the form of a question to make sure you have understood the other person correctly:

"So you were trying to be nice to him, but he took it the wrong way and began yelling at you."

- Expressing the underlying feelings. We have an inkling of what the other person is feeling and we reflect that back: "That must have made you very angry."

These are basic skills one learns as a couselor but are helpful listening skills that can enhance anybody's communication. We all long for another person to truly listen to us. Too many people feel that they have not been listened to and experience this as a deep wound; those people may feel offended if you do not listen to them.

Listening is a skill that needs to be developed. People vary in their capacity to listen, but no matter how good our listening skills, it will enhance all our relationships if we can improve and refine this skill. Mindfulness enhances our capacity to listen. We also need to be free from emotional reactivity, because ER disrupts our capacity to listen to others. The first six steps in this book set the stage for non-reactive listening. By listening to others we model and teach others how to listen to us.

Validation

To validate another person is to let them know we not only understand their experience, but that they are acceptable and we are not judging them. There is no more powerful skill in helping others feel accepted and to help them calm down emotionally than validation. The confusing part of using validation is that sometimes what other people do and think seems wrong or distorted. How do we validate that? We don't have to agree with the person to validate them. One thing we can always do is validate the person's feelings. Emotional validation is important to do even when a person is getting upset about something that seems absurd to us. Emotions are facts and many people have a strong need to have their feelings validated. Validation is very soothing and helps people calm down when they are reactive or upset. If a person's upset is based on unreasonable assumptions, there is no way for them to reason it out until they are calmed down emotionally.

Validation is a primary tool in relationships, but many people do not know how to use it. It is important to be able to validate others who are close to us or with whom we work. Children need validation to be healthy emotionally and to have good self-esteem. Validation is important in marriages and in other family relationships in order for people to feel understood and appreciated. Most of us know how to validate children or validate people who are distraught. For instance, if somebody at our work is grieving due to the loss of somebody close to them, to validate their grief we might say, "It must be so hard for you to lose somebody you lived with and loved for ten years."

We can use validation to calm others down. It is helpful to validate the other person's experience until they start feeling better. This may take some time. Once this validation is completed and the person is calmer, then their rational minds begin operating again and the person can usually examine the situation more objectively. Validation is a way to help others move through their emotional reactivity more quickly.

It is usually effective to focus on the emotion that a person is experiencing. Examples of validating statements are: "That must have been really hard for you." "This is a very distressing thing to have happened to you." "I can see how you would be very upset by this." Notice that these validating statements remain fairly vague about the specific emotion that the person is feeling. We don't want to get it wrong—then the person may focus on correcting us rather than the emotional experience of feeling validated.

It is easy to be non-validating by ignoring or avoiding people who are emotionally upset. When we get emotionally reactive ourselves, there is no way to be validating to others. At that point we are too busy looking for validation ourselves. Some statements are particularly invalidating, such as: "You shouldn't feel that way." "Get over it." "That's the past, don't let it affect you." Any statements that give a person feedback about what they should change before they are able to calm down and talk about the situation is invalidating.

To validate someone's emotions effectively, one must be mindful. Sometimes we face a situation when an important person in our lives is angry with us and accusing us of something that is untrue. It takes a tremendous amount of mindfulness for us not to react. Even in the midst of this situation which we judge to be very unfair, the best thing to do is validate the other person emotionally. We may need to defend ourselves at some point, but there is no way for the other person to hear us until they are calmed down. Once they have calmed down then we can attempt to be honest and authentic about our side of the disagreement.

Honesty and Authenticity

The more important the relationship, the more important it is to be honest and authentic. We particularly need to be honest in the expression of our emotions because emotions are the currency of intimate relationships. If emotions are not expressed openly, there will be little intimacy. Even with important relationships at our place of employment, honesty is critical to success. Honest communication keeps operations in touch with reality. If your boss, employee, or fellow worker is moving in a direction that could be damaging to the organization, it is important that you find a way to bring up the issue. Good leaders encourage subordinates to be honest with them. Some even go so far as getting evaluations from their employees that list their weaknesses along with their strengths.

Before we begin giving others feedback or sharing something that will be hard for the other person to hear, we need to make sure the other person is calm. It is important to give specific and behavioral feedback, because vague feedback is easier to react to and is harder to profit from. Specific feedback about one's behavior feels less like it applies to one's character. Behavior is relatively easy to change, but character is not.

- An example of vague feedback that can be taken personally: "John, I wish you would help around the house sometimes." John can easily take this to mean he is not a helpful person, or that he never helps. This can seem to be an overwhelming problem to correct.

151

- An example of specific feedback in the same situation would be: "John, you told me you were going to vacuum today. Will you do that, please?" John now sees himself as only forgetting to vacuum. This seems much easier to remedy.

We need to stay mindful in these situations and attend to the person to whom we are giving feedback. If the other person begins to get upset, don't get triggered yourself. Stay vigilant of the sensations in your body so that you will know immediately if you are getting reactive. If the other person begins to be defensive, you may need to change your approach. It can be helpful to return to validation. This will encourage the person to calm down so that they can once again hear you.

Don't pile it on. Deal with one issue at a time. Remember that few of us have the strength to hear more than one or two criticisms at once. A slew of criticisms are easy for people to take personally, and then they may become defensive. Many behaviors can be changed rather easily if we are clear about what the behavior is and feel that it is within our power to change.

Honesty and authenticity not only apply to giving other people feedback, these also contributes to our ability to share what we are feeling and thinking. When we have a feeling we need to express it clearly. Remember it takes practice learning to sort out your feelings, put them into words, and then feel comfortable expressing them to others. It is a learning process that can be refined over one's lifetime.

Accentuate the Positive

Plants need soil, sunlight, water and carbon dioxide. Relationships need listening, validation, honesty, and positives. Relationships cannot thrive in an atmosphere of negativity, so make sure you express positives in your relationships. Honesty is not just about expressing complaints; it is also about expressing what you like about somebody else. There is a rule that has been used in marital relationships for some time: the six-to-one rule. One should express six positives for every negative in a relationship. Recent research has shown this to be true in work situations also. People need to know that you think that they are good, liked or respected. This is not conveyed to others magically; it must be communicated.

Children need to hear positives about themselves to grow up with good self esteem. Spouses need to hear this to know that they are loved and respected. Family members need to hear this to know that you care. Employees need to hear this to retain their morale and remain productive. Positives create an atmosphere of optimism, caring, and cooperation.

There are three basic ways to express positives: through appreciation, by compliments, and by expressing positive feelings toward others. When we express appreciation, we tell the other person that we appreciate something that they do. This can be anything from a simple thank you to a more involved description of what they do for us. "I really appreciate you making my lunch today." "Thanks for taking care of that paperwork yesterday. It's a load off of my mind."

Giving compliments is a closely related skill. We compliment people on how they look or act, some trait that they have. "You look nice in that blouse." "You have natural warmth that comes across to the customers." "I love that drawing you did, son."

Expressing positive feelings toward others can be a very straight-forward approach to expressing our emotions. Examples are: "I really enjoy spending time with you." "I have been looking forward to our chat this week." In more intimate relationships, expressions of feeling that are more personal are necessary for intimacy.

There is a wealth of evidence that expressing positives to others builds more positive bonds, yet some people never do this. There are numerous reasons for this. It is hard for people to do this if they have never received positives from others, particularly while growing up. They may feel uncomfortable and will have to practice to overcome that discomfort. Others may have trouble expressing positives because of built up anger and resentment. The person thinks that the other person does not deserve the positive. For instance, a woman angry that her husband does not give her presents may be loathe to show appreciation when he finally does give her a present. Unfortunately, if she doesn't show appreciation for his present, then she may not get many more. When we are resentful, it is best not to act it out. Talk about it. Express it clearly, and ask for a behavioral change. Don't let it stop you from expressing positives.

CHAPTER KEY POINTS

- When you reduce emotional reactivity, more opportunities to respond compassionately arise.

- All major religions encourage us to be compassionate.

- Attending to others and listening closely are skills that make it possible to be more compassionate.

- Validating others, giving honest and specific feedback, and accentuating the positive are great ways to enhance a relationship.

EXERCISES

1. Mindfulness of others: Sit down in a quiet room and choose an inanimate object to be mindful of, like a chair, plant, or desk. Sit directly across from this object. Start by attending to this object as completely as you can. If thoughts distract your mind, gently return your attention to the object. Once you have stabilized your attention on the object, notice your body and the sensations you are experiencing while you are attending to the object. When you are able to attend to both of these at once, bring into your field of attention awareness of the room as a whole. Try to be simultaneously aware of the object, yourself, the room, and your complete field of awareness at once. See if you can experience this global awareness when you are attending to others.

2. Choose a person in your life that you feel critical toward. This could be a family member, a friend or acquaintance, or somebody at work. Think of one thing they do that you can appreciate. Even if they just sweep the floor occasionally, you can appreciate that you don't have to walk on a dirty floor. Can you think of an honest compliment you could give this person on their looks, actions or personality traits? Try to come up with a number of appreciations and compliments for that person. How would it be to say one of these to that person the next time you see them?

3. How would you validate a spouse or partner in the following situation? Your spouse is upset with you because you are late

and did not call. You're sure that you told your spouse that you were going to be late. She or he is angry at you for something you feel is not your fault. Most people know how to defend themselves in this situation, but how would you validate your spouse in this situation? What are some validating statements? Focus on feelings. Don't validate facts you think are untrue.

4. Think about the person in the Exercise 2 that you feel critical toward. Try to come up with an exact behavioral description of what the other person does to irritate you. What would that be? Stay as behavioral and specific as possible.

5. Do you give the important people in your life six positives for every one complaint? Think about the people you care most about, and compare the positives you tell them to what you say to people you don't care about as much. Can you increase the amount of positives for all the people for whom you are not meeting the six-to-one ratio? If you feel it would be difficult to do this, explore why this is true.

CHAPTER 9

The Components
of an Emotion

"If you work at the parts, the whole will be a success."
UNKNOWN AUTHOR

The Five Components of an Emotion

An emotion can be broken down into a number of distinct components. Learning to identify these parts aids us in becoming skillful
at handling our emotions. Failing to understand that our emotions have
a number of parts is one of the major reasons we have problems with our
emotions. In this chapter we will see why that is so. We can't understand
our emotions if we see them as just one unit. It's too simplistic. It's like
knowing that our car has an engine, and trying to fix the car on that basis.
We need to know the different parts of the engine and what they do to
be a competent mechanic. The five components that apply to emotions

159

in general also apply to the dysfunctional emotions that we experience when we are emotionally reactive.

There are five basic components* of an emotion: feeling, sensation, behavior, thinking, and how personally we experience a situation. In this chapter, we will explore these components so that we can learn how an emotion functions. Having a deeper understanding of emotions can help you to utilize the techniques for dealing with emotional reactivity presented in this book. These techniques are based upon working with these different components.

Feelings

The first component is feeling. Each emotion is characterized by a particular feeling in our body. Feelings are typically positive, negative or neutral. The feeling component is one of our main ways of knowing whether something is either pleasant or unpleasant. Because the feeling element is so prominent in any strong emotion, we may easily think that emotions and feelings are the same thing. We also may use the words interchangeably. Feelings are subtler than emotions. We are feeling all the time. When we walk into a room, we have a feeling response to the room and its décor.— we like it or don't like it. The feeling response to the décor of a room is not typically considered an

---

* Although there are many definitions of emotion and ways to look at emotion, here I will focus on the components that are within our awareness to change and that we can most easily benefit from therapeutically. Other components such as chemical changes in the body and brain are interesting and can help our general understanding of emotions, but they are not directly accessible to our consciousness.

emotion. However, we could become emotional about the décor of a room if we felt strongly enough about it.

We have feelings about everything. They tell us whether we like, dislike, or are neutral about what we are experiencing. They also tell us something about the quality of our experience. If you are standing on a busy street corner in a big city, the feeling experience you have will be qualitatively different from standing in a forest. Feelings communicate subtle information about our environment.

There is a feeling component in every emotion. We typically dislike the experience of "negative" emotions such as anger, shame, guilt, sadness, or fear. We like experiencing positive emotions such as joy or love. When we experience neutral feelings, there is no accompanying strong emotion.

The qualitative aspect of feeling helps us experience our emotions more fully. If someone betrays us, we may say that it feels like that person put a dagger in our heart. We probably have never experienced actually being stabbed, but we imagine that it has some of the same qualities. We make many of our decisions in life based on this qualitative aspect of feeling. We are drawn to situations that make us feel good and repelled by situations that make us feel bad.

When we are under the influence of strong emotions, our bodies react, flooding us with intense feelings that can interfere with our functioning in a situation. The feeling component can be so strong that we may use fiery language to describe what we feel; "I felt so in love, I was on fire." "He was so angry that it was as if a terrible storm had descended on him." An intense enough emotion can be felt in every cell of our bodies. This can be so stimulating that it becomes difficult to think and act appropriately.

The feelings we experience when we are emotionally reactive are similar to feelings felt during any intense emotion. The difference is that we are projecting our past onto the present. With emotional reactivity the feeling component tends to become exaggerated. A situation that we would normally respond to mildly takes on high arousal, because the situation triggers something that has happened to us in the past. This makes it more difficult to handle the situation, and our reactions are likely to become more extreme. They become inappropriate for the situation.

A feeling can be so strong that it fills up our awareness. It is difficult to attend to anything else. The positive or negative value of our feelings can also become extreme. We hate feeling the way we do when somebody injures us, so then we "hate" that person. We love the feeling of being in love. Intensity of feeling can become so prominent that we may overlook the other components of emotions. When we are emotionally reactive, the feeling component becomes more exaggerated and unpleasant than is appropriate to the situation.

Sensations

A component closely connected to feeling is sensation. Strong emotions trigger physiological changes in our bodies that create sensations. Adrenalin and other chemicals stimulate us, and blood flows to or away from different parts of our bodies. All this creates sensations, and these are occurring on a cellular level. We may have very similar sensations whether we are experiencing fear or excitement—a rapid heartbeat occurs with more adrenalin pumping through our body. Yet excitement will *feel* positive and fear negative, while the sensations may be pretty similar. Sensations are more objective and discrete than the feeling component. We can enhance our contact with an emotion by identifying the discrete sensations experienced. Bringing our sensations to awareness can help us experience our emotions more fully, and because sensations are physiological rather than psychological, we contact an aspect of emotion that is less distorted by preconceived notions and former experiences.

Behavior

Besides the feeling and sensation components, all emotions have a motivational or behavioral factor. When upset, there is pressure for us to respond in some way, typically with fight-or-flight behaviors. If we love somebody or are attracted to them, we want to approach them; if we hate somebody or find them disgusting, we want to distance ourselves from them. Most emotions have a motivational component. Usually, the stronger the emotion, then the stronger the need is to act. The difference with emotional reactivity, compared to healthy emotions, is that our behavior can easily become an overreaction to the situation. It is also pre-programmed which allows little room for choice. When our buttons get pushed the behavior comes out; if we are angry we yell; if we are afraid we withdraw. Our behavior becomes mechanical like a Coke machine.—push the button and the Coke comes out. With emotional reactivity, we lose our flexibility in responding and overreact to situations, or act in ways that are not in our best interests.

Thinking

All emotions have a cognitive or thinking component. We must have information before becoming emotional. For instance if someone dies in our family, we do not feel grief until we get the news. We may have never felt jealousy until somebody tells us that our spouse is cheating on us. Once we are told this information, we experience jealousy whether it is true or not. Later, if we find that our spouse is not really cheating on us, our jealousy may disappear completely.

As we can see, it is important that our thinking is correct about a situation. We do not respond to an event but to our interpretation of that event. That interpretation is based upon how we think about it. For instance, after a bombing, a terrorist group may be overjoyed that they have been able to successfully kill innocent people to further their "cause". Almost all other people would interpret the same event differently and be appalled by the violence and loss of innocent lives.

When we have difficulty with our emotions, the thinking part is distorted and irrational. For instance, when we hear the news that a friend has died the bad news naturally triggers sadness, but some people increase the negative emotion. They imagine that they will never have a close friend again. This assumption may increase their grief and lead to a sense of hopelessness or even depression. When we are emotionally reactive, we are distorting information in some way. There are numerous cognitive distortions that can be involved with ER. Either the person is thinking irrationally, in an exaggerated fashion, or in a way that makes assumptions about the situation or the other person that distort their responses. These false assumptions and distorted views are a central feature of emotional reactivity.

How Personally We Experience a Situation

Taking things personally stimulates our emotions and reactivity. Although, personalizing is technically a part of our thinking, it is such a prominent component in our emotional life that it is fruitful to deal with it separately. How emotionally we react to a situation depends on how close to home it hits. The more personal it is to us, the more potent the emotion. If you see an obituary of somebody that you never met, there will be little emotion involved in reading about it. If an acquaintance of yours passed away, you may feel more emotion; a friend's death would elicit more, and a very close family member intense emotion. The more we deem a situation as personally meaningful, the greater the emotion.

Some people take everything personally. Their thinking is distorted in that they believe that they are the center of other people's actions. These people are the most emotionally reactive. For instance, the boss, Mr. Jones, comes in very upset and angry one day, and Sarah reacts very personally to this. She thinks that something she did may be responsible for Mr. Jones's mood, and fears she may lose her job.

She becomes very angry with Mr. Jones, thinking that he should not go around with a bad mood affecting everybody else at the job. In contrast, her coworker, Lisa, does not take what is happening to Mr. Jones personally in any way. She assumes that Mr. Jones is in a bad mood and this has nothing to do with her. Because she does not personalize Mr. Jones's bad mood, Lisa does not find herself getting emotional about the situation. She has a much more peaceful day than Sarah does. People with a habit of personalizing become more emotional in general, and reactive to events and other people.

Emotional Reactivity Has the Same Five Components as Any Emotion

Emotional reactivity has all the components of normal emotions: feeling, sensation, thinking, the tendency to personalize, and the urge to behave in a certain way. When we are emotionally reactive, these components become exaggerated and out of sync with reality. Distortions in thinking increase the likelihood that we will act in dysfunctional ways, and this raises the arousal level of our feelings and floods us with too much stimulation. This makes it difficult to think clearly and to act responsibly. The high arousal of the feeling element, the destructive behavior, and the faulty thinking all feed on each other, exaggerating our responses and leading to a loss of control of our behavior. This is what makes ER so painful. One of the goals of this book is to put forth methods that are effective in eliminating emotional reactivity and changing it to normal emotional responsiveness. Throughout the book we have been discussing these components and learning how to deal with them

Regardless of how they manifest, either in healthy or dysfunctional ways, all emotions have these basic components. This is an important point because people may think that the acid test of whether or not they are in touch with their emotions is solely based upon how much they are in touch with the feeling component. Awareness of the motivational-behavior element, sensations, and the thinking component is ignored. It is not enough to strongly feel our emotions to be fully in touch with them. It is necessary to be aware of all five aspects of our emotional life.

Understand These Components and Lessen Reactivity

It is imperative that we be able to discriminate between these aspects of emotion to be able to handle them appropriately. Dr. Murray Bowen, one of the founders of family therapy and the person who first developed the concept of emotional reactivity, stressed the importance of being able to discriminate our thinking from our feelings. He saw this as one of the criteria of emotional maturity. People who have confusion in this area show more emotional reactivity. Cognitive-behavioral therapists also emphasize the distinction between thoughts, feelings, and behavior when discussing how emotions are expressed. They stress identifying the thinking element and then changing our distorted thinking. Changing our distorted thinking creates a change in the resulting emotional reaction.

These five components each demand a different response from us. If we respond to our emotions as one undifferentiated mass, we make it difficult to handle them. Some components demand a very active approach and need to be changed, while other components need to be accepted and experienced fully. We need to have an active relationship with the behavioral, thinking, and personalizing components of our emotions. We examine these components, see if they are appropriate, and then change them directly if they are distorted or not working for us. We need to make sure that these components are not dysfunctional. We must question our behavior to see if the behavior is appropriate to the situation. By questioning our distorted thinking we can make sure our emotions are based on reality. We can notice if we are taking things more personally than is necessary. Unfortunately, many of our judgments about situations and our behaviors have become automatic and unconscious. We need to pay attention to them so we can exhibit choice in how we act and how we think. By choosing our behaviors and ways of looking at situations, we can make sure that our emotions are more manageable and less painful.

The feeling and sensation elements in an emotion demand the opposite response. An appropriate relationship to the feeling and sensation elements is to be receptive — to allow ourselves to experience them fully. Sensation and feeling do not need to be questioned or changed. Emotions need to be fully experienced. We need to bring our unflinching awareness to our feelings and sensations and allow them to rise fully in our consciousness. This full acceptance of the feeling element gives the emotion the capacity to do what it is meant to do — to move. One of the roots of the word "emotion" comes from the Latin, *movere*—to move. If we respond to all five of these components properly, we set the stage for a deeper understanding of emotions and develop a capacity to handle them effectively.

Awareness of these Components Can Help You Master Your Emotions

Unfortunately, most people are unable to discriminate the different components that compose an emotion. They try to handle all of the components of an emotion the same way. Some people are more concerned with their thinking and behavior. They are aware of how their thinking has been distorted or how much their behavior has gotten them into trouble when they were highly emotional in the past. They believe that the best way to deal with their emotions is to question them and change them. This works well with the behavioral and thinking components but has terrible consequences when applied to the feeling and sensation components. We cannot directly change our feelings and sensations. We can only suppress them. This approach can lead to denial of the feeling element, emotional numbness, and a lack of connection with the sensations in our bodies. This incomplete approach gives the person some control over their emotions, but they pay the high cost of not experiencing their emotional life fully.

Others are very aware of the importance of embracing the feeling element, and they are very good at experiencing their emotions intensely. Unfortunately, they apply this accepting quality to their thinking and behavior, too. They feel their emotions very strongly but never question their thinking, which may be irrational. They also may never question their behavior, which may be inappropriate. These people are lively because they are in touch with the feeling element of their emotions, but they have overwhelming problems in their relationships because their behavior is based on distorted thinking. Many times these people have had a history of being talked out of their emotions or told not to feel so deeply. This has made them feel like they have to defend their emotions. On some level they understand that their feelings need to be accepted but they apply this to their behavior and their thinking also. Because of their confusion about the different components of emotions, they not only defend their healthy emotions, but they also defend their emotional reactivity with its inappropriate behavior and distorted thinking.

If we are confused about our feelings and emotions, this confusion will negatively affect our closest relationships. It is not uncommon for people to fall into either the "emotional" or the "rational" camp. Very emotional people, who are emotionally reactive, defend their strong emotions. Others who are very rational about their emotions, are tightly controlled, and tend to be unemotional. These two types are naturally critical of each other. The highly emotional type feels that the mentally controlled type is not very lively and is unfeeling. The mentally controlled type thinks the other type is too emotional and irrational. They are both wrong and both right.

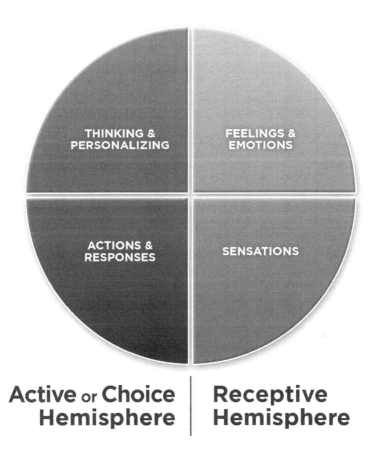

Active or Choice Hemisphere | **Receptive Hemisphere**

An emotion contains all of the above components. The components on the left side of the diagram are components that can be directly changed through our action. They need to be questioned for their appropriateness and rationality. The components on the right side of the diagram cannot be changed directly. They need to be embraced or held in our awareness and to be felt fully. Responding to the components on each side of the diagram in the appropriate way helps reduce emotional reactivity. Thinking and personalizing are grouped together because personalizing is a type of thinking.

Diana is angry at John because he will not move toward setting a date for their marriage. Diana becomes so angry that she becomes abusive toward John when they talk about this issue. This behavior makes John even more hesitant about getting married to Diana. When John asks Diana to try to change her destructive communications, Diana becomes immediately resistant. She interprets John's request as a request to stuff her feelings and accept that he is never going to marry her. Diana has been told to stuff her feelings before in her life, and when she did this it was painful. She felt very inauthentic. Her view of emotions is not sufficiently differentiated. She does not realize that she can question her thinking and behavior without giving up the experience of her feelings. Once Diana learned that she could do this, she was able to remain honest about her feelings of rejection, and at the same time express this in a different and more effective way to John.

Dale had the opposite problem. His wife, Heather, complained that he never talked about anything that was personally affecting him. At times, when upset, he would withdraw and not talk much. Dale's previous experiences with emotional expression were not positive. His parents were out of control with their emotional reactivity. His father had a serious anger problem and his mother was emotionally upset much of the time. As a teenager, Dale started feeling better about his life when he learned that he could change his negative emotions to some extent by thinking positively and not letting others, including his parents, get him down. This stance toward his emotions helped him to become less overwhelmed and more functional in his life. When Heather would ask him to express more emotion, John assumed that this was a request for him to give up behaving rationally and to quit thinking things through. John's lack of understanding of the different components of emotion inhibited him from being receptive to feelings and sensations, which are prime components of emotional life. This led Dale to shut his feelings down and lose touch with his body. When Dale began to understand his emotions and their components, he was able to relate to his emotions in a more open way. He realized that by allowing himself to feel, he did not have to give up his rational mind, or to behave dysfunctionally like his parents. This helped him open up more to the feeling aspects of his emotions, and also helped him get more in touch with his body.

Cultural Confusion About How to Handle Our Emotions

Not recognizing the different components of emotions has led to confusion culturally in how to deal with them. One extreme is the rationalist demand to control our emotions at all cost. This inhibited way of living was the hallmark of the 1950's. In the 1960's, pop psychology began to encourage us to swing to the other extreme — to feel and express our emotions, not considering the rationality of our thinking or appropriateness of the behavior expressed. These confused views of our emotions continue to the present day with many people still advocating these uninformed, extreme ways of handling emotions. Luckily, there has been a more quiet inquiry into the nature of emotions among psychologists and philosophers that has led to a better understanding of what makes up our emotional life. Seeing emotions as having a number of different components is based upon some of these wiser considerations.

Schools of Psychotherapy Based on These Components

This confusion about emotions has led to schools of psychotherapy that have focused on one or another of these components, while excluding the others from consideration. The behaviorists focused almost exclusively on the behavioral component of psychological problems. Little attention was given to the cognitive dimension of experience and none was given to feeling. Emotions were considered to be too irrational to qualify as a scientific area of study. Various emotional release therapies (like Primal Scream) focused on the feeling component. Cognitive therapy, until recently, focused exclusively on changing distorted thinking as a means to recovery. Therapies that focused on one component were found to be limited in their ability to help a wide range of individuals. In the last few decades, more integrated views and therapies are becoming popular. They are more effective because they take into consideration two or more of the components of our emotions.

Re-educating Ourselves Emotionally

There are three basic methods through which we act in our world. The simplest one is reflex. This is purely instinctual. It allows for very little flexibility. The response of a doctor hitting our knee creates a jerk that is pre-determined and rigid. The most flexible response system we have for determining our actions is through deliberative thinking. We can think about a problem and decide carefully how to act. The thinking system, however can be slow. It can take a long time for us to make a decision and act. The emotional system lies in between these in terms of speed and flexibility. When we learn something emotionally, we can respond quickly. We can act in a situation that looks like a previous one without having to think it all through. This quickness of response by the emotional system can save our lives in dangerous situations. The emotional system is not as flexible as the thinking system, however. We can react inappropriately to situations.

We have no need to change or re-educate the reflex system. The intellectual system can be difficult for some to modify. If we have opinions that are in error, it may take us time, energy, and openness to rethink our opinions and have them better match reality. We are familiar with the re-education processes that we use to change faulty thinking. They are learned (for better or worse) through our educational system.

Unfortunately, most people lack the awareness of how to re-educate their emotional systems. When our emotional learning is faulty, we end up repeating the same dysfunctional ways of responding again and again. Many times we know that we are acting inappropriately, and yet we feel unable to change our behavior. We try to re-educate ourselves by convincing ourselves through logic, for instance, that we shouldn't grab more chocolate when we are feeling depressed about our weight. Trying to impose the way we change the thinking system onto the emotional system will not work. We need another way to do this. Understanding this five-component model and applying it to our emotions gives us a tool to re-educate ourselves emotionally so that we can make the changes that are needed.

Being aware of the different components of our emotions is an important factor in their mastery. In general, understanding of our emotions is obscure at best; thus, people are left to their own devices to learn to deal with their emotions. This has led to poor results. By discriminating clearly between the components of emotions, we can move very rapidly toward the goal of becoming adept at managing our emotional lives. You will find that the techniques outlined in this book are much more effective than previous suggestions of how to manage emotions because they are based on a multi-component view of emotions.

CHAPTER KEY POINTS

- An emotion can be broken down into five components: feeling, sensation, behavior, thinking, and personalizing.

- To overcome emotional reactivity, we need to change our behavior, thinking, and tendency to personalize, but we need to accept and allow the feeling and sensation components.

- Not understanding these different components of an emotion leads to confusion and conflict in how to manage emotions.

Exercises

Remember an emotion that you recently experienced. See if you can break it down into its components: feeling, sensation, thinking, behavior, and how much you personalized the situation. The following questions can help this exploration:

1. What was the feeling tone of the emotion—positive, negative, or neutral?

2. Were you able to notice exactly what sensations in your body were triggered by this emotion?

3. What were you thinking during the situation? Was your thinking accurate or distorted?

4. How did you behave? Did you act on the feeling? Was this action the most appropriate for the situation?

5. Was the situation very personal for you? Did you take the situation more personally than you needed to?

CHAPTER 10

What causes emotional reactivity?

"You know that sick feeling that comes over you when you and your husband are shouting angrily at each other—and then you look up and see your child standing wide-eyed in the doorway?"

MARION WINIK

There are many causes of emotional reactivity. Distorted thinking and lack of understanding of our emotions have already been mentioned as contributing factors. Painful interactions with parents and other prominent figures in childhood also contribute to emotional reactivity in adulthood. This includes experiences of sexual, emotional and physical abuse. Normal emotional learning is disrupted by these experiences. It is important to understand, however, that emotional reactivity is too common in the population to only be caused by clear-cut examples of abuse. Many people can't point to a clear memory of abuse in their lives, yet they grow up to be emotionally reactive. It can be instilled in children in subtler ways than through obvious abuse. Most parents have their own difficulties with emotional reactivity, and they pass it down to their children in one way or another. All strong negative emotional experiences in our lives have the capacity to make us susceptible to emotional reactivity. Genetic factors as well as ignorance about our emotions also contribute to this susceptibility.

We Learn to Deal with Emotions from Our Parents

Murray Bowen, who originated the term "emotional reactivity," said that people generally have the same level of emotional reactivity as their parents. Because our parents form the environment in which we grow, they have a profound effect on our emotional development, both consciously and unconsciously. We learn how to deal with our emotions from our parents more than from any other source.

Very few people grow up in homes where there are two emotionally mature parents. Unfortunately, most of us have emotional deficits and pass these down to our children as they were passed down to us. In large groups, I sometimes ask the question if anyone has grown up in a family where they considered both parents to be emotionally mature. Usually only a few people raise their hands, if any.

In early childhood our parents provide everything for us on a physical level. They also look out for our emotional needs. When we are infants, good parents provide emotional soothing when we get upset. When we feel hurt, a good parent will hold us and soothe us until we calm down. Through this soothing, repeated over time, we learn how to soothe ourselves. We gain confidence that our emotions are manageable through the process of being soothed by our parents. A parent who is not emotionally reactive has the natural capability of providing this service to her children. Healthy parents know how to soothe themselves, know how to handle their own emotions, and pass these skills down to their children.

Emotionally reactive parents have difficulty soothing their children. Because ER is catching, the child's upset may trigger the parent's emotional reactivity. The upset child will trigger a withdrawal reaction or irritation in the parent. This creates a disruption in the parent's ability to soothe the child. The infant misses the opportunity to learn a needed skill from the parent. Instead of the child learning soothing from the parent, the child learns to be emotionally reactive from the parent.

Recent research in early childhood attachment between parents and children indicates that a child's development is affected by how attuned a parent is to their child. When a parent is attuned to an infant, the parent responds to the emotion that the child is feeling at the time and reflects that back to the child in an appropriate way. The child is given a sense that what they are expressing to the parent is important. It is nearly impossible to be attuned to our children or anybody else when we are emotionally reactive ourselves. Lack of attunement can even affect the physiological development of the brain in a growing child. If we can avoid emotional reactivity as parents and can attune ourselves to our children, we will encourage our children to develop the capacity for handling their emotions in a healthy manner.

If children do not receive the proper soothing and attention when they are upset, they become more upset in the hopes of receiving the attention that they need. If parents are not responsive to the child and soothe the child quickly, over time the child may develop a habit of needing to get very upset to receive the attention they need. Rather than learning self-soothing skills from a parent, they learn emotional reactivity. This habit can follow them into adulthood.

The second way children mimic their parents' level of ER is through modeling. The child learns this even when not directly interacting with the parents. Throughout the child's upbringing the child witnesses how the parents handle various highly charged situations, and he learns these methods from them. Let's say that the father is emotionally reactive and expresses this aggressively. The son will learn from the father to either express his anger the same way, or he will become fearful of anger and avoid it. Getting angry or withdrawing becomes the habitual way he deals with emotionally charged situations.

The child of an emotionally reactive parent ends up with a similar level of reactivity as the parent. The close interaction during infancy and throughout childhood determines to a great extent positively or negatively how the child will learn to handle her or his emotional arousal.

John was not directly abused in his childhood, but his parents fought frequently. When his parents fought, John feared that his family would break up through divorce. During their fights each of his parents would threaten to leave. Occasionally, his father would leave for a day or two after one of their fights. This reinforced John's fear of separation and abandonment. To get away from this distress, John would usually leave the house and take a walk when his parents began to argue. In nature he found a peace that he could not find in his home.

As an adult, John continued to avoid conflict. As soon as he and his wife became embroiled in an argument, John would immediately leave the house, take a drive to his favorite hiking trail, and think things over until he calmed down. He would not return home until he was sure his wife had calmed down, too. John's experiences in childhood had deeply conditioned him. He never saw his parents resolve a conflict, and thus he did not believe that he could resolve a conflict with his wife. He felt his only hope was escape. Only by working on this matrix of avoidant behaviors, distorted thinking, and high emotional arousal was John able to overcome this knee-jerk tendency to run from conflict.

Emotional Reactivity May be a Result of Abuse or Neglect

Emotional reactivity is typically formed during high states of emotional arousal. We learn to deal with emotions from past experiences of strong emotion. High arousal of emotion occurs in response to abuse and neglect. Children are sensitive to distress in many situations that adults are not. Direct abuse is one of the most potent factors in conditioning a child to become emotionally reactive, because abuse arouses some of the highest levels of negative emotion possible.

Parents who abuse their children typically do this when they are also experiencing high levels of emotion. Some parents would never choose to be abusive if they were thinking clearly but lose control during states of emotional reactivity.

Intense emotional reactivity needs three ingredients for its creation. One is strong emotion. This is the fire in which ER is forged. When there is abuse, there is high arousal of negative emotion. In the midst of the strong feelings of abuse, the child is given negative messages about the world, themselves and others. These distorted beliefs are the second main ingredient and form the cognitive part of ER. At the same time, the child searches for a behavior that will reduce the uncomfortable feelings. The type of behavior selected varies according to the temperament of the child. Typically, these action tendencies are variants of fight, flight, or freeze. These behaviors are the third ingredient in the formation of ER. These beliefs and behaviors become deeply associated with the powerful feelings that occurred at the time. The intense emotional situation provides the fire to fuse the feelings, the behavior, and the beliefs into one pattern. This pattern expresses itself again and again throughout one's life.

Let's take the example of Jake. As a youngster beginning in fifth grade, Jake was picked on incessantly by a few of the other boys at his school. Jake was a sensitive child and was easily overwhelmed by emotion. When the other boys picked on him, he would begin crying and shaking, and the other boys enjoyed their power in getting Jake to react so painfully. In middle school Jake became very ashamed of what he thought was weakness in response to the other boys' teasing.

The shame eventually became greater than his fear of violence. Finally, he couldn't stand it any more and began to lash back. He found that fighting, even if he lost, was preferable to feeling overwhelmed. He vowed never again to experience the sense of shame he had suffered previously. Jake developed a hair-trigger for violence.

Jake's fear of vulnerability became fused with his belief that it was better to fight or even die than feel shame again. This belief also fused with the behavior of violently striking out at his opponents. This led to a problem for him with emotional reactivity throughout his life that ultimately landed him in prison. This did not change until he began therapy to work on his emotional reactivity and his anger management issues.

Ida's experience was much different. She was a shy child. Her mother teased her about her shyness. It was particularly painful because her mother did this in front of others, and this exposure was very mortifying for her. In school, when she was required to give a presentation or speak in front of the whole class, she felt very vulnerable. She found that certain behaviors would help her to avoid having to experience this. She would become sick before any class presentation to avoid going to school. To make the work up, she would do something else that she could do alone, like writing a paper. In later life, anytime that Ida felt exposed in social situations, she would immediately find an excuse to leave the scene. As an adult, she had few friends or positive social encounters.

For Ida the heat of emotion that set the stage for her emotional reactivity was the deep humiliation experienced in her younger years with her mother and at school. She believed that if she allowed her vulnerability to show, others would make fun of her. Her habitual behavior was to avoid situations or leave them immediately when any sense of embarrassment surfaced. This emotional reactivity became so deeply fused in her that it was very difficult for her to react in any other way, even though she wanted more friends.

Traumatic events can happen at any time in life—not just in childhood. Whenever they happen they condition us to be emotionally reactive. This conditioning is subconscious because we are not aware as infants what affect our parents' emotional reactivity is having on us. When we are abused, we are not aware of the negative beliefs and behaviors that are being programmed into our subconscious. Because these reactions are programmed so deeply into our psyche, we are only capable of reprogramming ourselves when we become conscious of the original emotional matrix again. Hopefully, with the help of the information in this book, times of emotional reactivity can give us an opportunity to explore these areas in our psyche and heal them. Using emotionally reactive situations as an opportunity to heal deeply held trauma is discussed in Chapter Twelve.

Conditioning by Repeated Experiences of Emotional Pain

Emotional reactivity is not always formed by obvious childhood abuse. Small irritations experienced over time can create emotional reactivity. For instance, in Virginia's marriage, her husband Ken has a habit of leaving his clothes on the bedroom floor. Initially, she ignored this.

However, it became a bigger and bigger issue for her. Now when she sees his clothes on the floor, she gets extremely angry. Her reaction has become exaggerated considering the smallness of this event. She begins to over-personalize Ken's habit of leaving his clothes on the floor.

It is like getting a sliver in the foot. What was once a small irritation becomes more and more irritating the longer we walk on that foot, and eventually we can think of nothing else but getting the sliver out. We stop focusing on the fact that the rest of our body is fine. Unfortunately, many couples go through a similar experience. Small problems become so irritating that a couple fails to recognize that the relationship also has wonderful qualities. It is not unusual for the five percent of a marriage that is troublesome to take up ninety percent of the attention. Small issues not dealt with over time can contribute to emotional reactivity, at least in some relationships.

Genetic Predisposition Contributes to Emotional Reactivity

Psychologist Leslie Arens has studied very sensitive people, and in her book, *The Highly Sensitive Person*, she describes some of the difficulties these people have. The highly sensitive person has more sensitivity to stimuli of all kinds. They compose about 20% of the population. They are sensitive to sounds, may have difficulty sleeping, need more down time to unwind, need more time alone, etc. Because of difficulty in dealing with high arousal states, these people can develop an avoidant pattern of emotional reactivity. They anticipate that certain situations will be over-stimulating for them. They avoid these because they were overwhelmed in similar situations in the past. High arousal can feel uncomfortable for them, and they avoid situations where this may take place. The highly sensitive person is more likely to develop avoidant behaviors as an expression of their emotional reactivity.

For the person with low sensitivity to stimuli, boredom is an issue. They seek out highly stimulating circumstances because they feel generally under-stimulated. These people may have more of a predisposition to become addicted to the fight side of the fight-or-flight reaction, engaging in conflict with others as a means to continue to that stimulation.

Stress Exacerbates Emotional Reactivity

Each individual varies in the amount of reactivity they have day-to-day depending on how much stress they are under. There is a recognized association between stress and anger. Gridlock on Los Angeles freeways has created so much stress for some people that they have threatened other drivers with guns. Stress affects people's fight-or-flight reaction because people commonly withdraw or get angry under stress.

It is helpful to be aware of the numerous stressors that can affect us. Hunger can be a stressor. A person with low blood sugar can be prone to irritation and emotional reactivity. Other factors include tiredness, overwork, worry, and not taking time to relax or do something enjoyable in one's life. Sometimes, we run into periods where a number of problems occur in our life at the same time. For instance, a person with marital problems, who has job stress, and who experiences a death in the family may become very susceptible to emotional reactivity, and the tendency to withdraw or become irritable will be much greater at such times. If you are more stressed out than usual, it is helpful to practice mindfulness more diligently to ensure you don't succumb to emotional reactivity.

Women experiencing pre-menstrual syndrome (PMS) can become particularly vulnerable to emotional reactivity during this part of their cycle due to changes in serotonin levels in the brain. Although these changes are purely physiological, they can lead to deep sensitivity in the emotions. During the pre-menstrual phase, a woman may feel that containing her emotional reactivity is like riding a bucking bronco. Women may benefit from practicing mindfulness during this time of the month. Mindfulness is an excellent way to contain the emotional reactions to these strong physiological changes.

We have many experiences in our lives that affect us and can contribute to the creation of emotional reactivity. It can be very helpful for us to understand how we have become so reactive. This can give us a clearer sense of how to change and can help us work through the underlying feelings associated with the emotional reactivity. However, for some, it may not be necessary to know where it came from. The important thing is to consider how our own emotional reactivity expresses itself now. We can then apply the techniques presented in this book to develop more healthy methods of dealing with our emotions. Learning skills to deal with our emotional reactivity can be a major cornerstone in helping us heal from past trauma.

CHAPTER KEY POINTS

- Emotional reactivity is largely passed down from our parents. We learn how to handle our emotions from our family.

- Abuse and neglect cause us to be emotionally reactive.

- Repetition, stress, and genetic predisposition all contribute to emotional reactivity.

EXERCISES

1. When you were growing up, were your parents both emotionally mature? How well did your parents express their emotions? Were they able to express a wide range of emotions freely and appropriately?

2. Consider some of the events in your past that were highly charged emotionally. Do you think that these events conditioned you to be emotionally reactive when similar events occur now? What was the emotion that you felt then? Did you form any beliefs about yourself or your life from that event? Did you develop any behaviors in response to that event in your life—that have now become habitual when you get upset in similar situations?

3. Notice your level of stress, and how it changes over time. Do you find that you are more prone to emotional reactivity during these times? Practice mindfulness of the body during these times and see if it helps you manage your stress and your emotional reactivity.

CHAPTER 11

Fear of Emotions

"When it comes to emotions, even great heroes can be idiots."
Sir Te, commenting in the film
Crouching Tiger, Hidden Dragon, on the inability
of the hero and heroine to express their love to each other.

Suppressing Our Emotions Contributes to Emotional Reactivity

There are two basic problems that people have with their emotions. The first is difficulty in controlling the inappropriate expression of emotions. This type of ER occurs when we are overwhelmed by our emotions and then act in ways that are not in our best interest. It is a common phenomenon and is the most obvious type of emotional reactivity. All we need is the right situation to trigger us. We get our buttons pushed and this leads to the fight part of the fight-or-flight response.

The second basic problem that people have with emotions is the tendency to repress them. When we repress our emotions, we lose contact with them and no longer know what our feelings and emotions are. Repressing our emotions not only sets the stage for emotional reactivity, but contributes to many other difficulties as well. Repression leads to the flight response because we become avoidant of situations that can trigger our emotions. When we repress things long and hard enough, we come to a point where we express our emotions unconsciously—they leak out. Sometimes repression backfires and a person can swing to the other extreme and have uncontrollable outbursts of emotion.

Why Do We Avoid Our Emotions?

Strong negative feelings and emotions can be unpleasant, and focusing on them increases our awareness of their unpleasantness. It becomes tempting to turn away from our feelings and distract ourselves from experiencing them. We avoid unpleasant feelings because they can be painful.

Many people have had difficult experiences with strong emotions. Negative strong emotions like rage, hurt, and fear occur at the worst times in our lives. When we allow ourselves to experience these feelings, we are reminded of these painful past events. The feeling becomes the trigger that brings the whole event back to us. If you feel rejected and allow yourself to feel it fully, it may remind you of every rejection that you ever had. Because negative feelings are a pathway to many of our most painful moments, we are tempted to avoid our feelings so these painful memories are not re-triggered.

Negative emotions can also be connected to situations where we behaved badly, and this can add to the fear we have of our feelings. If the last time I got angry, I said or did something I regretted, then I may avoid anger at all costs. I am certain that if I get angry again, I may alienate someone else. If the last time I felt shame, I acted foolish or weak, I may be afraid to experience shame or embarrassment again. I become ashamed of my own feelings, because I can't handle them very well and others can see this. By numbing myself to these feelings, I hope to never be embarrassed or vulnerable again.

This overriding fear can become so intense that we will do almost anything to avoid uncomfortable emotions. We may use drugs or alcohol to numb ourselves, or even seek out fear-inducing activities, flooding our bodies with enough adrenaline to drown out other emotions and becoming addicted to an adrenaline "high." Some individuals sacrifice the experience of falling in love. They avoid the feeling because it arouses too much vulnerability. Opening to this positive feeling would open the gate to negative feelings such as loss or rejection. Others may design their lives with routines that avoid all situations where negative emotions might be triggered. Their lives become limited and feel lifeless. They develop elaborate excuses for not stepping outside their circle of comfort.

Society does not encourage us to feel our feelings. "Don't be so emotional," or "She gets upset too easily," are common sentiments in our society regarding people who are "too much" in touch with their emotions. Each culture has specific emotions that are considered acceptable to express. Almost all cultures encourage positive emotions like happiness, and discourage negative emotions like anger. In the United States certain emotional expressions are discouraged—displays of affection are uncomfortable for many Americans.

Some societies in the past were particularly repressive regarding specific emotions. In the Victorian era in Europe, sexual feelings were considered to be unacceptable. In the prudish medical texts of the time, it was considered an unfortunate fact that men had sex drives, but considered acceptable and necessary for procreation. For women, sexual feelings were thought to be unnatural, and if a woman had sexual desire, she was labeled perverse. As a consequence, it was difficult for women to deal with their natural, sexual feelings, and this led Freud to conclude that sexual issues were behind every neurotic symptom. In his day and age, this was actually the case much of the time.

Gender roles can also limit our capacity to experience our emotions. The feelings that are acceptable for men in American society are still limited, although it has been improving slowly. Because society tells us that men are supposed to be tough, vulnerable feelings have been off-limits for men. The list of vulnerable feelings is quite extensive and includes: hurt, grief, shame, guilt, sadness, and fear. This makes it difficult for men to fully accept themselves. It contributes to the obsessive concern some teenagers have in looking tough—anything not to appear vulnerable. When you deny your own vulnerability, you do not respect it in others, either. This perceived lack of permission to experience vulnerability contributes to male violence in our society. Many men feel they have to convert every vulnerable emotion to anger, which appears stronger and more "masculine".

For women, the main feeling that is taboo is anger. This is very apparent to most women. When I ask a group of women what name they will be given if they express anger, in unison they invariably chime, "bitch." This strong societal proscription against anger makes it feel dangerous for women to admit even to themselves when they are angry. This can make it very risky for women to assert themselves. The consequences for denying our feelings are potent, and this lack of support for feeling anger has severe negative consequences for women.

Avoiding Feelings Leads to Defenses and Symptoms

There are numerous and varied pressures on us not to experience our full range of feelings. Unfortunately, when we fear our emotions, we have to establish elaborate ways to avoid them. These ways of avoiding are our defenses and symptoms. If we have strong emotions that we believe we are not entitled to feel, then we will have to find strong means to avoid them. One of the most effective ways to avoid feelings is through the creation of dramatic symptoms.

When Freud was in Vienna, he worked with women who were deathly afraid of their sexual feelings. They developed elaborate symptoms to deal with their sexual repression. Freud named this neurosis,—*hysteria*— a common psychiatric diagnosis in his era. Symptoms such as fainting, depression, and psychosomatic illness were a result of the repression of sexual desire. When a woman was able to discuss her sexual or other emotions openly and come to terms with them, the symptoms would disappear. By accepting the emotions she had been repressing, her symptoms were no longer necessary. Thus Freud developed what he called the "talking cure".

This relationship between symptoms and repression of feeling is still a common experience in psychotherapy. Interestingly, sexual feelings have become much more acceptable and typically are not the feelings that the person in our society represses. The hysterical reactions that were common during Victorian times are uncommon these days. Feelings such as guilt, shame, anger, grief, and hurt commonly underlie our neuroses in the modern world. Let's look at some of the common areas in which symptoms appear in a person's life.

Areas of Our Lives Affected by Repressed Emotions

Emotions expressed in the body

Some people excel at repressing their emotions and not acting them out in other areas of their lives. The emotions have nowhere to go, so they are expressed through bodily symptoms of various kinds. They affect muscle tension, and exacerbate other illnesses such as ulcers, spastic colon, and all stress-influenced diseases. One of my clients, in his initial session with me, presented with a psychosomatic problem.

He came in with a stiff neck, and it was difficult for him to move it without intense pain. As he began talking about the difficulties he was experiencing in his life, he sobbed. He cried for at least twenty minutes. At the end of the session his neck loosened up and was not stiff at all. This scenario repeated itself for a few more sessions until he began to work through his personal problems. As he learned to talk about his feelings, the problem with his stiff neck disappeared. He was a prime example of how repressed emotion can directly affect a physical problem.

Massage therapists, Rolfers and other body workers report this connection between repressed emotion and tensions in the body. It is not unusual for a massage therapist to be working on a knot in someone's back and find that as the knot loosens and relaxes there is a corresponding emotional release, usually tearful. There is also evidence that letting our emotions out can affect our health in other ways. In one study it was found that terminally ill medical patients who joined a group where they could discuss their feelings had fewer complications and better health than those not in such a group.

Taking our emotions out on ourselves

Many people lack the skills to productively work through their emotions. They do not have the capacity to totally repress their feelings, and hurting somebody else is not an option for them, so they take their emotions out on themselves. A dramatic example of the self-destructive symptoms that may develop is with people who cut or burn themselves. Individuals who self harm are usually conscious that they are cutting because they cannot deal with an emotion that feels overwhelming. They relieve their negative feelings by cutting or burning themselves. In one of my first conversations with a "cutter," she described the painful buildup of emotion leading up to her wanting to harm herself, and then the immediate relief she felt after cutting her arms or burning herself. The physical cutting is the symptom related to the unpleasant emotion. It's as if the physical pain of the cut or burn replaces or distracts from the emotional pain.

This phenomenon is also apparent in drug and alcohol addiction, which is so destructive to one's body and to one's life in general. Many addicts trace a direct connection between escaping uncomfortable emotions and their use of drugs or alcohol. One reason drug use works so well is that the intoxicating substance is distributed throughout the whole body, covering up the sensations of any unwanted emotions with those of alcohol or drug intoxication. Many kinds of dramatic, destructive behaviors may be used to avoid experiencing our unwanted emotions.

Indirect and passive-aggressive expression of our emotions

This is a common way for people to channel feelings that are repressed. Al is frustrated by his employer's rude treatment of him, but is afraid to directly confront his boss. He tries to forget it and "put it behind him", because he is not very skilled at asserting himself. He ends up expressing his anger by criticizing his boss to his co-workers behind his boss's back. Another indirect way that one can choose to express anger is through displacing it onto others. Al returns home to his family and criticizes them for not straightening the living room. His frustration with his boss leaks out through his unwarranted criticisms of his wife and children. Al may believe that the true reason for his upset is the living room, but fails to connect his anger at his boss with his criticisms of his family.

There are all sorts of indirect ways that our feelings can express themselves. Unresolved emotions can be expressed through dreams. It can be interesting to pay as much attention to the feeling tone of our dreams as it is to the images. For instance, violent dreams are often connected with unresolved anger.

Direct but inappropriate expression of emotion

Emotions can be expressed directly through violence, abuse, or some other destructive means. Usually in these situations, the person is very aware of an emotion such as anger, but they express it inappropriately. The person appears to be in touch with their emotions because they are expressing them so directly. Actually, they have allowed their anger to take them over. They are aware of their anger, but avoiding underlying emotions such as hurt and fear—emotions that are less comfortable for them.

Direct and appropriate expression of feelings

Being aware of our feelings and choosing how to express them in the most effective manner is the only healthy kind of emotional expression. As humans, one thing that our highly developed frontal cortex affords us is the ability to consciously symbolize our feelings and emotions through language. To be able to be conscious of our emotions and choose an appropriate mode of expression is the sign of a mature person.

The Social Necessity of Being in Touch with Our Feelings

Lack of contact with our feelings can lead to grave consequences physically and psychologically, and can affect many areas of our lives. One such area is intimacy, because feelings are the currency of the transactions that take place in a relationship. When we are unable to be aware of and express feelings, our relationships will become cold or riddled with difficult symptoms.

The inability to express the emotion of love is a common plot device in many romantic movies. A teenage boy is enthralled with the most popular girl in his class, but comes to realize that he is really in love with the girl next door. A man has a difficult time saying, "I love you," to his girlfriend. Once he expresses it, the relationship can finally go deeper. Tender emotions and sometimes more unpleasant emotions need to be communicated in a relationship for it to be healthy. If small hurts build up in a relationship and are not discussed, it can create a wall between people.

Our health can be affected by our contact with our feelings. One truism of medicine is that many of our health problems are due to addictive tendencies of various kinds, such as overeating, alcoholism and smoking. Many people start using these substances to distract themselves from painful emotions.

Being aware of our feelings enables us to process information received from the environment, allowing us to identify what we like and don't like. Many intuitions come through our feelings, like hunches and other information that can be helpful to us. If you consider yourself a good judge of character, you may notice that you use your feelings about somebody to make this judgment. If we are out of touch with our feelings and emotions, we lose touch with an important source of information about ourselves and the world around us.

Being in touch with our emotions is one way to feel more alive. Many people seek out various art forms in order to experience the emotions they trigger in us. Music may make us feel more animated. If we are bored and put on a song we love, our boredom disappears. Many people seek feelings of terror by going to horror movies, or seek the sadness that a sentimental movie may provoke in them. Comedies on TV are avidly watched for the humor they provide. These entertainments can make us feel more alive. Imagine how lively people appear in Italy—a country that is accepting of strongly felt and expressed emotions—and compare that liveliness to a less emotionally expressive population like one from Northern Europe.

Our feelings indicate what we want in life. We are attracted to a potential mate though our feelings, because a mate needs to feel right for us, among other selection criteria. Our feelings are an important sensor that helps draw us to an appropriate person to love. To know what career to pursue needs to be informed by our feelings. Otherwise, we take the risk of not liking what we do for a living, which is a common problem in our society.

Feelings are necessary to be able to set appropriate boundaries. They give us information that tells us if our boundaries have been violated. It is not unusual for people to walk away from an interaction with a lingering feeling that something was not quite right about it. Only upon reflection do they realize that the other person was discounting them or putting them down. This information first came to the person through the nagging, negative feeling that lingered after the conversation.

Categories of Emotions

There are various categories of emotion that lend to our understanding of emotions and some of the difficulties we have with them.

Healthy emotions are based on reality

Healthy feelings and emotions are responses to our environment that help us cope with life. These emotions lead to solving problems and constructive action because they are based on what is actually happening. If I am confronted with a wild animal, my fear is an important motivator for me to run away or protect myself in some way. Being in touch with our feelings is necessary for survival and coping. If we lose somebody we are close to, it is natural to cry and express our grief; it allows us to go on with our lives. Emotions based on reality are important to our survival and our social functioning.

Emotions not based on reality

Besides responding to reality, we also respond emotionally to our imaginations. We can respond to our thoughts as strongly as we do to reality. For example, if we dream that a killer is chasing us, we may wake up in a sweat with our legs kicking, as if running away from the dream killer. Sexual fantasy is another example of our bodies emotionally responding to our imagination; when we dream of having sex with someone, our physical bodies can become orgasmic. If we worry that we will not have the money to pay our rent, our bodies will be subject to the stress of that worry. Whatever we think, our bodies have the potential to respond to it emotionally

We can draw faulty conclusions about our lives and respond emotionally to them as if they were true. For instance, we may assume that somebody at our workplace is "out to get" us". This can provoke all kinds of feelings of anger and fear. The assumption that the person is out to get us may not be true, but we end up suffering with negative feelings because of this misperception. The tendency to think in distorted ways is what cognitive behavioral therapy is based upon. How we talk to ourselves, and what we believe about our lives, are strong determining factors of our emotional reactions. By changing our thinking and seeing things more realistically, we relieve ourselves of unnecessary negative emotions. Distorted thinking is one of the primary causes of emotional reactivity.

Manipulative emotions

These feelings are under our conscious control; they are used for the manipulation of others. This could be a positive manipulation, as in the case of an actor performing for our viewing pleasure, but can also be for a negative motive. Children may compare their parents' behavior to other parents in order to trigger guilt in them. "All the other kids my age can stay out later than I can. You are so mean!" If parents allow themselves to be manipulated, the child is rewarded, in this case by being able to stay out later. This reward will increase the child's tendency to manipulate in the future. Parents also use emotions to manipulate their children. "Guilting" one's children or intimidating them to get them to obey are examples of this.

Adults can use seduction to manipulate. One person expresses love for another to attain sex or money, but the "love" is put on as an act. One person pretends to be deeply hurt to make another feel guilty. A man goes into an angry tirade to intimidate another into giving him what he wants. Con artists are experts at manipulating others' feelings, but it is a fairly common behavior for many people.

Habitual emotions

Some people develop affinities for certain emotions and express these emotions habitually. Habitual emotions are used to distract from emotions that are more uncomfortable. Angry defensiveness is a common example of a type of habitual emotion. If you criticize me for doing something wrong and I don't want to feel the guilt, shame, or sense of failure that this accusation brings up in me, I will get angry and defensive. The feeling of anger makes me feel more powerful and less vulnerable than these other feelings. Because anger can be so intense, it works well to distract me from more vulnerable emotions.

Happiness can become a habitual feeling in our culture rather than a real one. We can downplay other, more difficult emotions by adopting a smile or actively cracking a joke. Sometimes people convert feelings to tears. Whenever they are confronted by challenging events, they break into tears. The crying becomes a cover for anger, fear, or some other emotion. Habitual feelings can be used to cover up pervasive feelings of emptiness. "I don't know what my feelings are so I'd better be angry. At least then I'll feel alive." The person who feels empty inside may create all sorts of dramatic situations that create painful feelings. This gives them an opportunity to feel that they are truly living.

A person may begin by using an emotion in a manipulative way, but it becomes habitual later on. A child may work himself into a tantrum to get what he wants from his parents. If he does this often enough, and is rewarded, it may develop into habitual anger which is difficult to change.

Habitual feelings over time become deeply associated with our sense of self. They become part of us and seem necessary for us to function in the world. Many clients I have worked with were initially unwilling to give up a habitual emotional response because they saw it as part of themselves. Giving up the distorted negative emotion felt to them like giving up who they were as a person. If a habit has been there long enough, it is hard to imagine life without it.

Unresolved emotions from the past

This type of emotion is intimately involved with emotional reactivity. Many times we do not have the opportunity to work out painful events when they occur, and we are left with a residue of the emotion. This becomes an emotional wound. We have covered it over but it continues to fester and hurt, particularly if it is touched.

When I worked in a substance abuse treatment program, I met John who lost his mother twenty years ago. At the time she died, he was using alcohol and drugs heavily, and he had continued to use for the last twenty years. Now he was suddenly sober, and when he talked about his mother, he responded as if the death occurred yesterday. John had never fully dealt with his grief in the past because he covered it over with substance abuse. Once sober, John was able to experience his grief and get over the loss of his mother.

Most people have deficits in dealing with their feelings, and have had traumatic events happen in their lives that they were not emotionally capable of handling at the time. When we are confronted with similar situations, these feelings are triggered again. Emotional reactivity has a large trauma component. We project the old emotion onto the new situation.

Experiential Avoidance

Recently psychologists have coined a term that is useful in understanding this tendency to avoid our feelings and other experiences. "Experiential Avoidance (EA) is the attempt to avoid or control one's internal experiences, including thoughts, emotions, and physical responses or the situations that might elicit these experiences" (Hayes, et al, 1996). Psychologists have shown that experiential avoidance plays a part in many mental health problems. EA is associated with anxiety, worry, panic, depression, and poor post-traumatic adjustment. Painful emotions are one of the primary experiences that people avoid.

Animals that are shocked in a laboratory develop avoidant behavior. Their behavioral repertoire becomes very limited because there is nothing that they can do to avoid the shocks. The animal's only recourse is to shut down and shut out the painful feelings. People are similar. If we experience something painful and overwhelming, we withdraw. We shut down in that area and hope we never experience it again.

People with serious mental health problems usually have high levels of experiential avoidance. The more we avoid areas of our experience, the more difficulties pile up. However, the more we embrace our experiences, the more behavioral flexibility and choice we develop, and the healthier we become.

Experiential avoidance is a factor in anxiety disorders. People with anxiety disorders experience distressing levels of anxiety and find ways to avoid this feeling. One way to do this is to avoid situations that cause anxiety. For instance, people with agoraphobia will avoid going into crowded places. Every time they avoid crowds, they receive a little reward for that avoidant behavior—they don't have to experience anxiety. Unfortunately, following this path may lead to a severe problem—the tendency to avoid can take over one's life. There are people with agoraphobia who no longer feel safe leaving their bedroom.

In depression a similar process may occur. A person does not feel comfortable with a specific feeling; this could be anger, grief, shame, guilt or any other negative emotion. The negative emotion remains in the psyche—avoided, yet still beneath the surface—eating away at one's happiness. Because a depressed person is unable to manage these feelings or to face events that might trigger this emotion, the person feels stuck and hopeless. Grief is probably the most common emotion avoided by depressed people.

Every mental illness has an element of experiential avoidance associated with it, which contributes to some of the challenges of treating mental illness. When the symptoms become painful enough, the person may seek help and, hopefully at that point, have enough motivation to face the experience more directly. When the client does this, they are more likely to recover.

Everybody, to some extent, exhibits experiential avoidance. For some it leads to mental illness, and to most of the rest of us, just limitation in our lives. The cure always includes recontacting the parts of our psyche that we have ignored. Psychotherapy reconnects individuals to areas of their psyche that they have avoided or repressed. No part of our psyche or our day-to-day experience should be off limits to us.

All effective psychological treatments incorporate some method of opening up and exploring our experience. One of the best ways to do this is through mindfulness. When we are mindful, we are not avoiding our experience. Instead, we are deeply in touch with our lives, sensing each bit of data. By remaining non-judgmental and curious, mindfulness nurtures an attitude of acceptance toward whatever life brings.

It is important that people have the skills to contact their pain without falling apart. Developing skills such as mindfulness, cognitive skills that help us think reasonably about ourselves, and skills in communication is necessary to make sure that we can manage our negative emotions and other difficult experiences.

For Individuals with Post Traumatic Stress Disorder

Emotional reactivity is a present reaction to a past painful event. If you have been severely abused, the emotional reactivity that you experience can be profound. The methods put forth in this book can be very helpful, but if while reading this you are triggered strongly and feel overwhelmed, consider one or both of these options. You may want to stop reading or thinking about this until you feel less overwhelmed. It may also be in your best interest to seek psychotherapy from a professional who is experienced in working with trauma. The self-help techniques that are described in this book are very helpful for the average person who is dealing with emotional reactivity. For those with post-traumatic stress disorder, more help and more time may be needed to work through these more serious difficulties.

CHAPTER KEY POINTS

- People have two basic problems with emotions: letting them get out of control or avoiding them.

- Fear of emotions and the vulnerability one feels when emotional can lead to avoiding them. Avoidance of emotions leads to symptoms and defenses.

- Emotions that are not experienced directly are expressed indirectly and harmfully.

- There are five categories of emotion that are helpful to understand: healthy emotions based on reality, emotions not based on reality, manipulative emotions, habitual emotions, and unresolved emotions from the past.

EXERCISES

1. Have you ever used manipulative emotions to get others to give you what you wanted? Think back to your childhood. Have these manipulative tactics been used on you?

2. Do you have emotions that are habitual or favorites of yours? Of the following emotions, think about which ones you are most and least comfortable with: anger, hurt, grief, love, joy, shame, guilt, and fear. Are you comfortable with feeling them fully? How comfortable are you in expressing each?

3. Think back to a time when you had a strong emotion that you were not expressing or did not know you had. How did you feel when you expressed it and got it "off your chest."

CHAPTER 12

A Door to Deeper Healing

> *"Healing is a matter of time, but it is sometimes also a matter of opportunity."*
> HIPPOCRATES

The Psychological Benefits of Working with Emotional Reactivity

We gain many benefits from being able to cope with the situations that push our buttons. The most apparent effect is that our relationships improve. Without emotional reactivity getting in the way, communication flows, and we are more confident in difficult emotional situations. It can improve communication in families and reduce abuse. Research suggests that being less emotionally reactive may have health benefits. If you have an addiction problem, it can help eliminate one of the

215

most common triggers to relapse. We suffer less unnecessary emotional discomfort. Decreasing ER can also have effects on the societal level by reducing crime and diminishing conflict in political situations.

Family relationships and marriages are particularly affected by emotional reactivity. ER is an interesting concept in that it straddles two worlds. It is a personal problem that we carry from our past, yet is also a family problem because it occurs in relationships. How emotionally reactive we are directly affects our success in having deep, abiding relationships. One's level of emotional reactivity is a simple way of assessing success in future relationships. People with high ER have trouble managing the subtleties of intimacy and parenting.

In my therapy practice, I have seen people reduce their emotional reactivity in a relatively short period of time. All they needed to do was to focus attention on this area and apply the skills in this book. My client, Martha, was very reactive to her boyfriend, Clark. Initially, she would fill most of the session with complaints about Clark. Her main complaint was that Clark could not be there for her emotionally. Martha stated this by saying, "Every time I'm upset, I want Clark to work it out with me and reassure me. Instead he backs off and shuts down." I asked Martha why she stayed with Clark if he was unable to meet her needs. She said that she had come up against this problem in past relationships. She wanted to work it out with Clark, rather than leave like she had with previous lovers. I reminded Martha that it was impossible for her to fix Clark, but she could work on herself and specifically her emotional reactivity. She agreed to do this. Over the course of about eight sessions Martha seriously tackled her emotional reactivity. She changed her behavior by eliminating the demanding tone with which she asked Clark to meet her needs. She worked on her distorted thinking by being more accepting of Clark's weaknesses, and she worked on her own feelings by embracing them.

By focusing attention on herself, intense feelings of abandonment began to surface. She learned how to soothe herself when these difficult feelings came up. She was able to reduce her emotional reactivity with Clark dramatically. Martha was amazed to discover that, through her work on this problem, Clark also had a radical change in his behavior. He again began to show support for Martha emotionally. He still, at times, would withdraw, but he would always come back after a short absence and renew his feelings of closeness with Martha. Because Martha was less emotionally reactive, he felt safer with her and no longer felt he had to protect himself from Martha's anger and criticism by withdrawing. With the confusion of emotional reactivity out of the way, Clark was able to respond with more love for Martha. Their relationship improved rapidly.

Martha started exploring unresolved abandonment feelings she had from her father. This was the source of her emotional reactivity, and her relationship with Clark became a door for her to resolve these old issues. The relationship between Martha and Clark went from having 90% of their time together conflicted to less than 10%. They began enjoying each other's company again. The love that they had experienced together in the beginning of their relationship returned. Martha thought that she was too damaged to have a relationship succeed, based on her history of unsatisfying relationships.

It was very gratifying to her to realize that she was not hopeless in her desire to have a healthy relationship. She just needed the right tools to deal with her problem. To pound in a nail you need a hammer; a screwdriver will not do. The hammer for Martha was dealing with her emotional reactivity.

Interestingly, I never met Clark, and yet I was able to help Martha's relationship with him without doing any direct marital counseling with the two of them. Although, as a couple, they still have problems to work out, by reducing their emotional reactivity they will be able to work through other issues with greater ease. In the meantime, they are having more fun in their relationship.

Working on emotional reactivity for some people can be like a magic bullet. John Gottman, who did research on marriages and why they fail, was able to identify four negative traits that destroy marriages. He could predict very accurately if a marriage would succeed or fail in the next few years by whether these traits were present or not. The first was criticism. This happened if one spouse attacked the other spouse's character, rather than simply complaining about specific behaviors. The second was contempt. This was a form of discounting the other person's feelings, ideas, desires, etc. The third was defensiveness, and the fourth was stonewalling. When a person stonewalled, they withdrew from the relationship by not attending or engaging in meaningful dialogue. Interestingly, all four of these are manifestations of emotional reactivity. By working on emotional reactivity, these four negatives in a relationship can be diminished immensely. The odds of a relationship being successful increase significantly.

Transforming Emotional Reactivity as a Personal Healing Opportunity

Transforming emotional reactivity has benefits that go beyond coping better with current situations. It can be used as a major healing opportunity in our lives. When we are emotionally reactive, we have a chance to re-experience a part of our emotional life that is ancient and has remained hidden from our view. ER is a door that brings us face to face with the emotions, behaviors, and beliefs that were set in childhood. This opportunity is unique because many people have difficulty accessing these deep wounds even in therapy. When we are emotionally reactive, these wounds come to the surface whether we want them to or not. By preparing ourselves, we can turn these moments of emotional reactivity from deficits to prime opportunities for self-healing.

It has long been understood among psychotherapists that to facilitate change, it is important that we contact a significant level of emotion. This explains the common therapeutic refrain of most therapists, "And how did you feel about that?" With this statement, the therapist is inviting the client to add the emotional element to their review of past incidents so deeper healing can take place. It is understood that without accessing one's deeper feelings, it is unlikely that deep-seated problems will change. Most therapists have had experiences of clients talking about deeply painful events in their lives, but doing it in a very non-emotional manner. I have had experiences of clients telling me about incidents of painful abuse as if they were reading the newspaper about an event that happened to someone else. When clients avoid their emotions, no healing takes place.

Two of the most potent means of change in therapy are to review past events in a thorough manner, and to work on one's feelings toward the therapist. The first is called "working through", and the second is "working through the transference." Working through the transference has always been considered, at least by psychodynamic therapists, as superior to "working through." Let's explore these in relationship to transforming our emotional reactivity.

As we noted, working through is considered necessary because a simple insight into one's problems is rarely sufficient to overcome deep-seated issues. Many people with emotional problems have received advice about what to change, and yet, they find themselves continuing with the same behaviors. Working through is considered a necessary step in therapy that takes a large share of the therapeutic time. It can take months to work an issue through. One essential aspect of working something through is exploring one's feelings about an event.

Using our model of emotional reactivity as composed of intense feelings, behaviors and beliefs, let's look at "working through", and then "working through the transference". One of the main parts of working through is to be able to stay with the feelings of an event that one has repressed or otherwise avoided. By bringing up the feeling, a number of things are accomplished. You can get comfortable with the feeling and learn to embrace it rather than avoid it. You can also explore the negative beliefs associated with the traumatic event.

When a traumatic event occurs, strong negative beliefs are instilled into the psyche; we may not be aware of the negative beliefs we retain from these situations. When we re-experience the negative emotions that the event brings up in us, the negative beliefs come up at the same time. We can review these distorted beliefs, then question, and change them. A dysfunctional behavior will have been fused into this mix, also. We have an opportunity to review our behavior and change it if the behavior is not appropriate. This behavior can be as simple as the knee-jerk reaction of avoiding an issue. Working through in the therapy process allows us to excavate and explore the original matrix of intense feeling, distorted belief, and dysfunctional behavior that was conditioned into us by the original trauma. Because we now can review the event and its emotional impact with a more mature understanding, we have an opportunity to respond differently.

In "working through the transference" the same thing occurs but with two added elements, projection and immediacy. The emotional upset with transference occurs when clients project their previous hurts onto the therapist. If your mother rejected you, then the odds are that sooner or later you will be afraid that the therapist will reject you, too. You project the relationship you had with your mother onto the therapist. This type of projection onto the therapist is called transference. What makes transference an especially good mechanism for *working through* is that the therapist is right there in the room. This gives the therapist an immediate opportunity to help the client see what is going on, take back the projection, and see the therapist in a more realistic light. This leads to a significant change in how clients see themselves and others. It gives them an opportunity to alter the original matrix of intense feeling, belief and behavior into something that is more flexible and functional. A deep relational habit can be changed.

Methods of transforming emotional reactivity as presented here can offer a third alternative for working through issues from childhood. Transforming ER has many of the same components as working through. The fundamental similarity is that when we are emotionally reactive we are in touch with the emotional intensity needed to create change. We step through a doorway that lets us relive a childhood issue in the present moment. These opportunities can be quite common if we are easily triggered. With working through in a therapy situation, it can take months for us to be able to access these deep feelings and work with them. By being prepared for situations of emotional reactivity, we can take advantage of these difficult times and use them for positive change.

Compared to working through in therapy, working with our emotional reactivity in a self-directed way has some advantages and disadvantages. One advantage is that it occurs without our needing to be in a therapeutic situation. If we are prepared to use the steps in this book, we can work on it anytime it occurs. Sometimes in therapy we may have issues that go unnoticed. It simply does not occur to us that these are problems, and the therapy process does not uncover them. With emotional reactivity, life events trigger us. Many of these we may not have anticipated as problematic. This gives us immediate access to important issues that need to be healed. We have a unique vantage point during times of emotional reactivity to see exactly how we behave and think at that moment.

Awareness of how we behave and think when we are emotionally reactive may not be available to us in normal states of consciousness. Only when we are triggered do these old patterns present themselves to us. Another advantage is that projection is a basic part of emotional reactivity. At the times we are emotionally reactive we are projecting onto the person or situation we are reacting toward. This gives us an opportunity to work on our projections, as is the case when we have transference to a therapist. It is also immediate like a transference situation. At the moment of emotional reactivity, we are projecting onto whomever or whatever triggered us right at that moment. By being ready and using our skills we can take advantage when the door to these childhood wounds opens. The purpose of this book is to give people these skills.

The disadvantage of working with our emotional reactivity as proposed in this book is that one does not have a therapist in the room to help the process along. Good therapists create an environment of trust that makes it safer to look at these issues and to face our vulnerability. A good therapist will encourage us to embrace our feelings rather than run away from them. They can help us see things in a less distorted manner, and help us review our behavior and find more effective ways to respond. All this is tremendously helpful.

The concepts and techniques in this book can prepare us to take advantage of times we are emotionally reactive. A time of distress and upset can change into one in which we can learn and grow. These methods can also be used either with or without a therapist, depending on each person's need, their motivation, and their readiness. If used in conjunction with therapy, these methods add to the therapeutic process, because a new way of working on accessing the deeper parts of the psyche becomes available. Attending to experiences of emotional reactivity can speed up the therapy process.

However, the average person who is sufficiently motivated and self-aware can put these methods into use and benefit from them, even if not in therapy at the time. The methods offered here are more deeply beneficial than most self-help methods because they work directly on issues that are not accessible in normal states of calmness. Their effectiveness is dependent on how well we get to know the techniques and how much we actually practice them at the times we are emotionally reactive.

These techniques are not new. They are taken from cognitive-behavioral therapy, relational psychotherapy, and Buddhism. The main Buddhist technique is called mindfulness and is being used currently as an adjunct by many therapists and therapies. If there is anything new in this book, it is the focus on emotional reactivity as a key to improving relationships and as a way to work on deeper issues. The book also specifies the techniques that are most effective in transforming this problem.

My hope is that you will be able to benefit from the information in this book. My experience with this information is that it can be radically effective in helping people. I have used it in marital, family, and individual therapy and have found it to be the magic bullet for many people. I have taught it as a class in a local graduate school and given workshops on this topic. Some of the people who have attended these workshops have told me that working with this material was a life-changing experience for them. I hope that this material benefits you in your life.

CHAPTER KEY POINTS

- Working on one's emotional reactivity can lead to healing deep emotional problems.

- Emotional reactivity creates opportunities to find those areas of our lives where we need healing.

- Using emotional reactivity this way has some of the characteristics of the therapeutic techniques known as "working through" and "working through the transference".

BIBLIOGRAPHY

Aron, Elaine N. (1997), *The Highly Sensitive Person*. Broadway Books.

Ben-Ze'ev, Aaron. (2001), *The Subtlety of Emotions*. A Bradford Book.

Bowen, Murray. (1993), *Family Therapy in Clinical Practice*. Jason Aronson, Inc.; First Edition.

Goleman, Daniel. (2006), *Emotional Intelligence: 10th Anniversary Edition; Why It Can Matter More Than IQ*. Bantam.

Gottman, John. (1995), *Why Marriages Succeed or Fail: And How You Can Make Yours Last*. Simon and Schuster.

Greenberg, Leslie S. and Johnson, Susan M. (2010), *Emotion Focused Therapy for Couples*. The Guilford Press.

Kabat-Zinn, Jon. (1990) *Full Catastrophe Living: Using the Wisdom of Your Body and Mind to Face Stress, Pain, and Illness*. Delta.

Linehan, Marsha, (1993), *Cognitive-Behavioral Treatment of Borderline Personality Disorder*. The Guilford Press.

Solomon, Robert C. (2003), *What Is an Emotion?: Classic and Contemporary Readings*. Oxford University Press.

Wachtel, Paul L. (2010), *Relational Theory and the Practice of Psychotherapy*. The Guilford Press.

AUTHOR
INFORMATION

Jim Piekarski is a licensed marriage and family therapist who lives in Southern California. He is the Clinical Director of Phoenix of Santa Barbara, a non-profit agency that treats adults with mental disorders. He also is a clinical supervisor for interns and trainees who are learning to become therapists at the Salvation Army Hospitality House in Santa Barbara. He has served as an adjunct professor at various colleges in the Santa Barbara area. *Mastering Your Emotions with Your Spouse and Others* comes from his experience working with couples, families and individuals over the last 30 years.